SONOMA COUNTY

PICTORIAL RESEARCH BY
NANCY J. HUTCHINS

"PARTNERS IN PROGRESS"
BY SUSAN CLARK

PRODUCED IN COOPERATION WITH
THE SONOMA COUNTY HISTORICAL
SOCIETY

WINDSOR PUBLICATIONS, INC.
CHATSWORTH, CALIFORNIA

SONOMA COUNTY

THE RIVER OF TIME

AN ILLUSTRATED

HISTORY BY

SIMONE WILSON

Windsor Publications, Inc.—History Books Division
Managing Editor: Karen Story
Design Director: Alexander D'Anca
Executive Editor: Pamela Schroeder

Staff for *Sonoma County: The River of Time*
Senior Manuscript Editor: Jerry Mosher
Photo Director: Susan L. Wells
Photo Editor: Cameron Cox
Senior Editor, Corporate Biographies: Judith L. Hunter
Production Editor, Corporate Biographies: Una FitzSimons
Customer Service Manager: Phyllis Feldman-Schroeder
Proofreader: Mary Jo Scharf
Editorial Assistants: Dominique Jones, Kim Kievman, Michael Nugwynne,
Michele Oakley, Kathy B. Peyser, Theresa J. Solis
Production Assistant : Deena Tucker
Layout Artist, Corporate Biographies: Bonnie Felt
Designer: Ellen Ifrah

Windsor Publications, Inc.
Elliot Martin, Chairman of the Board
James L. Fish III, Chief Operating Officer
Michele Sylvestro, Vice President/Sales-Marketing
Mac Buhler, Vice President/Sponsor Acquisitions

Library of Congress Cataloging-in-Publication Data
Wilson, Simone. Sonoma County : the river of time : an illustrated history/
by Simone Wilson ; pictorial research by Nancy J. Hutchins ;
partners in progress by Susan Clark.
p. 128 cm. 22 x 28
"Produced in cooperation with the Sonoma County Historical Society."
Includes bibliographic references.
ISBN 0-89781-326-X
1. Sonoma County (Calif.)—History. 2. Sonoma County (Calif.)—
Description and Travel—Views. 3. Sonoma County (Calif.)—Industries.
I. Hutchins, Nancy. II. Clark, Susan. III. Sonoma County
Historical Society (Calif.). IV. Title.
F868.S7W55   1990
979.4'18—dc20 89-29774   CIP

*FRONTISPIECE: Vivid fall colors form a lively mosaic of the wine country
and a hop kiln in this painting by Sonoma County artist Frank Gannon.
Painted over a 10-year period, this scene captures the essence and feel of the
beautifully restored Hop Kiln Winery. Listed with the National Register of
Historic Places, the vineyard was the setting for the film,* Lassie. *From the
Collection of Cynthia Lee*

*Page 6/7: One of four wine-growing regions in Sonoma County, the Alexander
Valley is home to many wineries. Other regions include Dry Creek, the Russian
River, and the Sonoma Valley. Photo by Patty Salkeld*

Contents

To my father, Francis Robert Wilson

Anybody can make history. Only a great man can write it.

—Oscar Wilde

Preface

Thomas Hardy once observed that "War makes rattling good history, but Peace makes poor reading." The saga of Sonoma County steers a course between these two extremes of upheaval and tranquility. Strife and intolerance played their part in the region's history, but so have long intervals of prosperity and growth, when people tended their fields and lived in harmony with their neighbors and the land. Men and women of character established farms and railroads, newspapers and towns, and their personalities shaped the history of the region. Even peace can make good reading.

Sonoma County, blessed with a mild climate and fertile river valleys, attracted waves of immigrants from all directions. The first Americans, crossing from Asia to Alaska, found their way here 5,000 years ago. Russians, Spanish, and Mexicans, extending their empires, met here and vied for control of the coastal lands. Forty-niners hurried to California to mine but stayed to farm. Europeans, Mexicans, and Asians, looking for work and a new life, staked out ranches, built railroads, planted vineyards. All of them left their mark on the country we now call the Redwood Empire, a land touched by beauty and resources. Here is the story of their hopes and endeavors through the years as history, the river of time, flowed through Sonoma County.

Acknowledgments

Any research project is a cooperative effort. I am indebted to the following people and organizations (and to many more) for their valuable help: To the Sonoma County Historical Society, especially Glenn Burch, Harry Lapham, John Schubert, and Mary and Adrian Praetzellis, for their cheerful assistance; to Professor Foley Benson of Santa Rosa Junior College, for insight into the life of native Americans; to Stephen Watrous, professor of history at Sonoma State University, for background on Fort Ross; and to Terry Wright, professor of geology at SSU, for telling me whose fault Sonoma County geology really is. Thanks to Audrey Herman for maintaining a priceless history archive at Sonoma County Library; to John Lofgren and Eric Nelson and the Sonoma County Museum; to Bo Simons and the Sonoma County Wine Library; and to the staff of Sonoma County Library for preserving the record of the past in books, newspapers, clippings, and photographs. I am indebted to the National Maritime Museum and the California Historical Society Library in San Francisco. Thanks also to Hugh Codding for anecdotes on the building boom; to Millie Howie for her expertise on wineries; to Ernestine Smith for memories of postwar Santa Rosa; to John Bigby for information on filmmaking in Sonoma County; to Mick Clumpner for enlarging my library; and to Toni Cannizzaro for proofreading and compassionate criticism.

Simone Wilson

This artwork, based upon written reports available in the mid-seventeenth century, depicts Sir Francis Drake being crowned by the American Indians during his brief respite on the coast of California. Courtesy, the Edward Von der Porten Collection

CHAPTER ONE

Legacy of the Past

Sonoma County, a land of rich valleys, rolling hills, and jagged coast, was born from the rough-and-tumble geologic forces of the Pacific Rim. Sliding continental plates, volcanic effervescence, slow erosion, and coastal uplift all helped shape the coastal ridges, the rugged shore, and the fertile plains. The Pomo Indians, the first inhabitants of northern and central Sonoma County, had their own explanation of the area's formation. In the early time, the earth was perfect. Even the coastline was perfectly straight, because it was made by Marumda the creator and his elder brother Kuksu to a degree of perfection unimagined in the contemporary world. But then Coyote came along and saw the straight coastline and decided that the earth, being perfect, really shouldn't be that way. So he made gigantic waves out on the coastline one day, and they smashed up the entire coastline of Sonoma County. But Coyote made the waves so big that one of them carried him out to sea and nearly drowned him. That's why coyotes don't like water, and that's why Sonoma County has a very rough coastline, because Coyote made it that way.

In another Pomo myth, Marumda and Kuksu were dancing in a sky house. When they were both good and sweaty, Marumda reached under his armpit, scraped out some muck and stuck it between Kuksu's toes. Kuksu did the same to Marumda, and as they danced the land oozed out between their toes.

This primeval tale of muck and motion isn't entirely at odds with the scientific version of geologic events. The bedrock of Sonoma County is the Franciscan formation, formed at the bottom of the Pacific Ocean 100 million years ago. These sediments smashed against the edge of the North American continent, becoming a jumbled mass of muddy sandstone. The dark layers look tumbled and folded, like a pile of wet clothes from the washing machine, maytagged into disarray. Sediments scraped off the floor of the Pacific piled up at the edge of the continent, forming coastal hills. The Russian River held its course as the hills rose, carving a vast watershed.

Other forces were at work along the San Andreas Fault and its branches like the Rodger's Creek Fault that runs directly beneath Santa Rosa and Healdsburg. The faults lend a north-south grain to the landscape. Rocks in fault zones were crushed, making them easy prey to erosion. Broad saltwater bays and lagoons formed in the depressions along the faults, leaving rich deposits. As the water receded, fertile north-south valleys were revealed that would one day nourish vineyards—Sonoma Valley, Alexander Valley, and the Santa Rosa-Cotati plain. Soils around Sebastopol, on the other hand, were laid down by an ancient sea; the resulting sandstone drains easily and makes the hills around Sebastopol ideal for apples.

To the east of the Cotati plain, magma rose to the surface, feeding a chain of volcanic mountains parallel to the coast. Its remnants are the Mayacamas Mountains and Mount Saint Helena, rising 4,344 feet to be the highest point on the eastern skyline. Hot magma is still heating water under the eastern hills. Settlers would build hot spring resorts there, and electric companies would harness escaping steam at the Geysers (which are misnamed—there are no spouting geysers at the Geysers).

With such dramatic geology, Sonoma County was destined to suffer earthquakes. During the 1906 quake the Point Reyes peninsula jumped 17 feet north, and buildings like the Fort Ross Chapel, built right on the fault, collapsed. Loose sediments underlying Santa Rosa shook like jello and devastated the town.

Before people arrived, the elements of future commerce were already in place. Basalt in the hills east of Kenwood would become paving stones in San Francisco. Vast redwood tracts in the northwest would build the city by the bay twice—in the 1800s and again after the 1906 earthquake. Rich soil was waiting for the grapes, apples, prunes, and hops that would nourish the world.

But long before towns, steam plants, and vineyards, the hills and valleys were home to cougar, elk, black tail deer, and the king of California animals, the grizzly that now remains only on the state flag.

Kyrill Khlebnikov, a Russian traveler reporting on the countryside around Fort Ross in the early 1800s, noted that "among quadrupeds the most important are bears, lynx, ordinary wolves, and small ones which the Spaniards call coyotes . . . They catch sturgeon in the Slavianka [Russian] River when the channel is open." Eagles, hawks, ducks, and loons soared over hills laced with redwoods, oak, and alder. Otters, whales, and sea lions swam the coast.

People came into this area as long as 5,000 years ago. Siberian parties crossed the land bridge that existed between Asia and Alaska 10,000 years ago during the last ice age. Their descendants gradually filtered down into all corners of the western hemisphere. Coast Miwok, related to tribes in the Sierras and the Central Valley, moved into Marin and southern Sonoma County around Sebastopol, Petaluma, and Bodega Bay. Pomo settled around Clear Lake and then moved southeast, claiming the Russian River drainage as well as the northern Sonoma and southern Mendocino coast. The Wappo lived on the county's eastern edge. The land was dotted with villages, some holding 1,000 people but most only a few dozen.

In their own memory, they had always lived there in the land prepared by the trickster/helper Coyote. According to a Miwok story recorded by Malcolm Margolin, Coyote gathered shiny black raven feathers, and as he walked along he laid a raven feather on top of each hill and named that place. On the following day, humans were living on every hilltop. Coyote told the other animal people, "Now that there is a new people, we will all have to become animals." Immediately all the animal people transformed themselves into birds and mammals and reptiles and insects as Coyote directed.

However they arrived, the first inhabitants gave names to their homes, and some of the names stuck after the Indian presence dwindled. Petaluma means "flat back," a reference to Sonoma Mountain. Cotati is Miwok for "a punch in the face," and Tomales comes from the Miwok for "west."

The Pomo are really six or seven distinct peoples grouped together by Europeans because of linguistic affinity. Pomo of the Russian River barely understood Pomo around Santa Rosa; Pomo languages were as distinct as German, English, and Norwegian. The Miwok spoke a totally different tongue, as different from Pomo as English is from Chinese.

The groups had many customs in common, however. Men stalked elk and deer, the hunter donning a deer skin and antlers and acting deer-like to creep close to his quarry. People went seasonally to streams for salmon and to the shore for mussels, seals, and salt. Women gathered three-quarters of the food, collecting manzanita berries, sap from sugar pines, and edible roots. Acorns from Tanbark oaks and Valley oaks were a prized staple. Women baked acorn meal into bread or cooked it as mush in a watertight basket with a hot rock, stirring occasionally to keep the rock from scorching the basket.

Although white settlers called California Indians "diggers," a derogatory term implying the Indians only ate roots and lived like animals, in fact the north coast Indians lived relatively well without overtaxing themselves or the land. With a warm climate and plentiful resources, the native Pomo, Miwok, and Wappo lived a life of comparative leisure, working only a few hours a day to provide all their needs.

"That left time for basketry, time for prayer, time for nothing at all, time for just being," comments Foley Benson, professor of Native American Studies at Santa Rosa Junior College. "The idea that the hunting and gathering cultures of California were on the verge of starvation, that they lived a bare existence hardly eking out survival, is not true. It's one of the mythologies that we have about them that has no validity."

Leisure time left room for games and artistry. Men played a sport like hockey with a hardwood ball, curved sticks and goal posts. During gambling games, each team sang constantly to distract the other side's players. Children played cat's cradle with string made of plant fiber.

Pomo and Miwok did not make ceramic pots, preferring lightweight watertight baskets for cooking. Pomo women achieved the most sophisticated basketry in North America, a tradition they keep alive today. They collected willow and pulled up long strands of sedge root from sandy stream beds. Some coiled baskets, woven as gifts, were covered in the bright feathers of mallards, meadowlarks, or blue jays, with flourishes of scarlet woodpecker crests. Miniature Pomo baskets, made for healing purposes, are the smallest baskets with designs ever made, ranging in size from two inches to the size of a pinhead.

The Pomo regarded natural resources not as commodities but as partners in harmony with man. They saw the salmon run and the acorn harvest as spiritual powers, and their ceremonies were designed to put man in the

OPPOSITE, TOP: This 1816 drawing illustrates Bay Area natives using a tule reed canoe, which was used to navigate coastal waters. Courtesy, The Bancroft Library

OPPOSITE, BOTTOM: The earliest inhabitants of Sonoma County included tribes such as the Pomo, Wappo, and Miwok, who lived well upon the abundant resources of the land. Courtesy, The Bancroft Library

BELOW: The Pomo kept in balance with nature, taking what they needed and limiting their population. One method of controlling growth may have been the sweat house, a communal lodge where the men lived away from their wives. Courtesy, Peña Adobe Museum

right relation to plants and animals. Without this harmony, the deer and salmon might be offended and remain aloof. The relation between hunter and hunted was one of reciprocal courtesy: The deer allowed itself to be killed; the hunter respected the animal's sacrifice by not wasting anything.

When whites arrived there were perhaps 8,000 Pomo in Sonoma, Lake, and Mendocino counties—not enough to deplete natural resources. Numerous customs kept the population low. Men lived away from their wives in a men's house, a semi-subterranean, communal lodge that served as a sweat house, where the heat of daily sweat baths probably inhibited sperm production.

In addition to the men's house, many communities had a Round House up to 70 feet in diameter for assemblies and ceremonies. Along the coast Pomo built conical dwellings of redwood bark; inland homes were made of grass or tule. The Pomo fashioned strings of shells for currency. Gathering shells from Bodega Bay's clam beds, they cut, drilled, and strung 200 beads at a time. Longer beads made from the thickest part of the shell were more prized, as were older beads polished through a lifetime of handling. Most valuable of all were beads of magnesite ore, which were baked until they changed from dull grey to bright red with colorful bands. Pomos traded these individually or used them as jewels in shell necklaces. By A.D. 1500 they were the prime suppliers of money to peoples farther east.

The first 50 centuries of Sonoma County history passed in relative abundance and isolation, until a day in 1542 when a Pomo on the shore collecting mussels might have looked out to sea, astonished to see a ship heading north. When Europeans discovered the existence of the western hemisphere in 1492, the two dominant sea powers lost no time in staking their claims to the unexplored and possibly lucrative territory. In 1493 Pope Alexander VI, with a stroke of the Papal pen, sliced in two this great terra incognita, with most of the Americas assigned to Spain and much of Asia to Portugal.

In 1513 Vasco Nuñez de Balboa stood on a hill in Honduras and viewed the Pacific Ocean; by 1520 Hernan Cortez had conquered Mexico and plundered its capital of Tenochtitlan. Rumors of Golden Cities, the so-called Seven Cities of Cibola, sparked land and sea expeditions from Mexico. But Spain sought another prize: a sea route to the Orient through the new lands, one faster and less hazardous than the treacherous passage Magellan found in 1520 at the tip of South America.

Sailors looking for these fabled Straits of Anian were the first Europeans to see the coast of California. Juan Cabrillo, sailing from New Spain (Mexico), cruised north along the coast, stopping at San Diego. Cabrillo died on his flagship, but his pilot Bartolome Ferelo took the ship north to Cape Mendocino, passing the Sonoma coast and surprising any native Americans looking out to sea. The first seafarer to land in the region, however, was the upstart English navigator Francis Drake.

The daring English mariner, with Queen Elizabeth's blessing, sailed from Plymouth in 1577 to plunder the lumbering Spanish galleons in his quick little ship, the *Golden Hinde*. Drake braved the Straits of Magellan and headed north along the Pacific coast, leisurely sacking Spanish ports in Chile and Peru and liberating a fortune in gold from the galleon *Cacafuego*. He then sailed north along the California coast, hoping to discover the legendary straits and scoot back to England.

No straits appeared, so Drake, with a leaky ship and a fabulous cargo, retreated south looking for a harbor to repair the *Golden Hinde*—and keep out of view of the Spanish. In June 1579 he dropped anchor in a sheltered bay and claimed the land for England. The voyagers named it New Albion, because "the white bancks and cliffes, which lie toward the sea" reminded them of their own English coast, wrote Drake's chaplain, Francis Fletcher.

The chaplain's description of the bay is vague, and because Drake's log was lost, no one knows for sure where

the *Golden Hinde* lingered for five weeks in the summer of 1579. Bodega Bay, Drake's Bay in Marin County, and even San Francisco Bay all have their partisans. Today most historians favor Drake's Bay—its white cliffs are the most striking—but Spanish mariners assumed his layover was in Bodega Bay.

Native people, most likely Coast Miwok judging from the few Indian words in Fletcher's memoirs, were fascinated with the white-faced visitors, whom they may have taken for spirits of the dead. The meeting was a friendly one with an exchange of gifts: English linen shirts for local feathers, quivers, and skins. Drake's party judged the Miwok to be a sturdy, good-natured people.

"They are a people of a tractable, free and loving nature, without guile or treachery," Fletcher wrote. "Yet are the men commonly so strong of body, that that which two or three of our men could hardly beare, one of them would take upon his backe, and without grudging carrie it easily away, up hill and downe hill an English mile together."

Drake's crew spent five foggy weeks in the harbor, where they got a taste of typical Sonoma coast summer weather: "During all which time," Fletcher lamented, "notwithstanding it was in the height of Summer, and so

ABOVE: After plundering a fortune from Spanish forts in Chile and Peru, Sir Francis Drake sailed his galleon, the Golden Hinde, *northward, eventually dropping anchor to make repairs in a secluded bay somewhere off the Northern California coast in 1579. Courtesy, Raymond Aker*

OPPOSITE: This engraving by Thomas de Leu depicts explorer Sir Francis Drake, who came ashore in Northern California on June 17, 1579, at the midpoint of his world voyage. The voyage began in November 1577 at Plymouth, England. Although brief, Drake's California sojourn was the first English encampment on the shores of the land that would become the United States. Here the first Protestant church service was held, and first English claim was made to this new land, which Drake named New Albion. Courtesy, Edward Von der Porten Collection

neere the Sunne, yet were wee continually visited with like nipping colds."

The English claim to New Albion was more a cocky gesture to nettle the Spanish than a practical conquest. England lacked the resources to challenge Spain near its Mexican stronghold. But Drake's claim strengthened Spain's resolve to colonize California. Sebastian Vizcaino charted the California coast in 1602, recommending Monterey Bay for an outpost since it was "the best port that could be desired, for besides being sheltered from all the winds, it has many pines for masts." Colonization began only in 1769, when Gaspar de Portola and Franciscan missionary Junipero Serra came north from Mexico. They passed by Monterey, reckoning it could not be the place Vizcaino had so enthusiastically described, and so pressed on to discover San Francisco Bay.

Lieutenant Juan Francisco Bodega y Cuadra, looking for San Francisco Bay after a voyage north in the *Sonora,* blundered into Bodega Bay on October 3, 1775, the first European to come to Sonoma County (with the possible exception of Drake). Indians, paddling out in tule canoes, "most liberally presented us with plumes of feathers, rosaries of bone, garments of feathers . . . " wrote Francisco Mourelle, the *Sonora's* pilot. As usual, the Indians were welcoming and the weather was not. Fierce tides buffeted the schooner, and its auxiliary boat "was broken into shivers."

Bodega y Cuadra anchored near the mouth of Tomales Bay, which he mistook for the outlet of a river, but his name eventually came to rest on the bay to the north. Later settlers mistakenly assumed the name came from *bodega,* the Spanish word for warehouse, because of a Russian storehouse built there in the early 1800s.

Loss of their landing craft prevented the *Sonora's* crew from coming ashore, so credit for the first land expedition in Sonoma County goes to a small party of

Spaniards. In 1776 the American Revolution was raging on the east coast, but in California colonization had only just begun. In October, while their colleagues were laying out the new presidio of San Francisco, Lieutenant Fernando Quiros and his pilot Jose Canizares took a small party by boat across San Pablo Bay and meandered up the Petaluma River, believing it would connect with Tomales Bay. They found no passage to the coast but explored the land around Petaluma.

An English captain, James Colnett, took refuge in Bodega Bay in 1790 and charted the area. Evidently he believed this was Drake's haven; Colnett identified his map as "a sketch by compass of Port Sr. Fs. Drake."

By then the Spanish government, seriously alarmed about Russian trappers and about the English at Vancouver, were determined to start an outpost north of San Francisco. Lieutenant Juan Matute came to Bodega Bay in 1794 with orders to start a garrison at the notoriously shallow bay. His ship, the *Sutil,* had a shallow enough draft to enter the harbor, but a follow-up ship from Mexico was too

Ivan Kuskov founded Fort Ross in June 1812 as the first Russian colony in California. The Russian Orthodox Chapel is pictured here. Courtesy, Sonoma County Library

large for the bay and had to return to San Francisco with its troops and supplies. When scouts reported the difficulties of building an overland route to Bodega Bay, the viceroy abandoned plans for the outpost. The coast was clear for the Russians to capitalize on the Spanish failure.

Russia coveted the Pacific Northwest as early as 1741, when the Bering Expedition to Alaska brought back 900 sea otter pelts, prized for their thick warm fur. Russian influence expanded in an arc across the northern Pacific from Kamchatka across to the Aleutians and the Alaskan mainland. Between 1745 and 1800 the lucrative fur trade spawned three dozen trading companies.

But hunters rapidly killed or dispersed the otter herds. By 1797 only a handful of competitors remained. They joined forces and emerged as the Russian-American Company, a private company which nevertheless had major supporters (not to mention stockholders) in the Russian Imperial Court. At its head in Sitka, Alaska, was Alexander Baranov, the kind of tough, independent trader needed to hold together a remote outpost. Baronov was lauded by Washington Irving as "a rough, rugged, hospitable, hard-drinking old Russian, a boon companion of the old roystering school."

As governor of the company from 1799 to 1818, Baranov faced two problems. He calculated the Russians had taken 100,000 otter pelts in the last decade of the century alone; the precious resource was vanishing from Alaskan shores. Also, starvation was a constant threat for the colonists. Alaska's growing season was short. The company's head office noted that "grain brought to the colonies from Siberia via Okhotsk is very expensive, and besides it is subject to loss because of frequent shipwrecks."

Baranov looked south for a solution to his headaches, especially after Count Nicolai Rezanov, a Russian Imperial chamberlain, ignored a Spanish embargo and sailed the *Juno* into San Francisco harbor in 1806. The Spanish, while officially aloof, were only too happy to trade for the *Juno*'s supplies—Flemish cloth, axes, sail cloth, and packets of needles. Rezanov in turn loaded up the *Juno* with Spanish wheat, lard, jerky, and garbanzo beans to take north to Sitka. Charming as well as bold, Rezanov cemented the amicable relations with the Spanish by becoming engaged to Maria de la Conception Arguello, the daugh-

Mission San Francisco Solano de Sonoma is shown as it may have looked in the 1820s. The "Great Adobe Church" (built 1827-1832) is believed to have been destroyed by an unexpected rainstorm while its roof was being repaired in 1838. It was replaced by the present building, which was constructed as a parish church by General Mariano Vallejo between 1840 and 1841. Courtesy, California Department of Parks and Recreation and James B. Alexander

ter of the presidio commandant. Rezanov stopped on his way back home to urge Baranov to expand into the unoccupied coast of Northern California. Traveling home through Siberia, he died; the unfortunate Maria waited faithfully for years before learning of his death.

After several successful hunting forays as far south as San Diego, Baranov sent his associate Ivan Kuskov to choose a site for a California colony. In 1809 Kuskov anchored in Bodega Bay, which he called Roumiantzof Bay. He set up a temporary post and explored the Sonoma coast, selecting a coastal bluff 10 miles north of the Russian River. Kuskov returned there in June 1812 on the schooner *Chirikov* with 25 Russians and 80 Aleuts in baidarkas (hunting kayaks) to found the fort of Ross, an archaic name for Russia.

To counter the Russian presence, the Spanish (and, after 1821, the new Mexican Republic) finally extended their influence north of San Francisco. The last mission— San Francisco Solano de Sonoma—went up in 1823, 11 years after the founding of Fort Ross. The Russian empire, moving south, and the Spanish empire, inching northward, came head to head on the soil of Sonoma County.

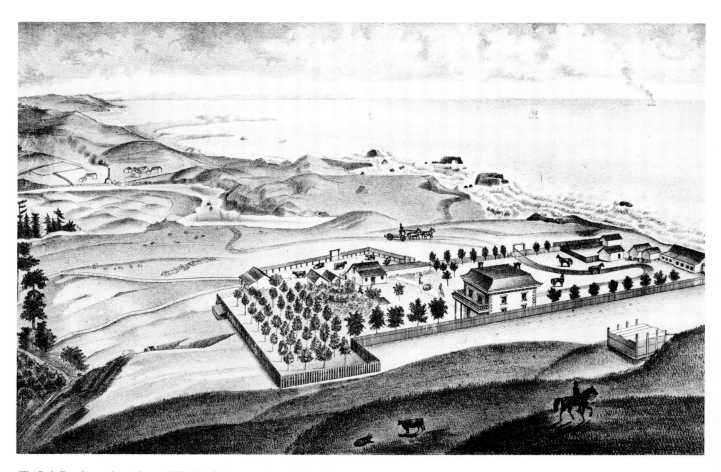

The Rule Ranch was the residence of Elizabeth Rule, a prominent citizen of Sonoma County in the mid-1800s. From Thompson, Atlas of Sonoma County, California, *1877*

Forts and Haciendas

The Russians and the Spanish—keen rivals if not exactly enemies— were in conflict when Russia established a southern base at Fort Ross on the Sonoma coast. The Spanish and later the Mexicans tried to discourage the Russians by forbidding them to hunt otters and by founding two missions north of San Francisco to block further expansion by the Tsar. On a person-to-person basis, however, relations were much cozier. No sooner was the Russian fort built than mission fathers came around to trade. According to Kyrill Khlebnikov, an officer of the Russian-American Company, "The local Spaniards were at first surprised to see these people, whom they had previously known only by hearsay and who lived in the stormy far off north, so close and so similar to themselves. All during the time the administration was corresponding with the Mexican Viceroy about the situation, the missionaries and other inhabitants became acquainted with their new neighbors and supplied them with livestock, grain and poultry, in defiance of their own government's prohibition of this very thing."

When the Russians first arrived in 1812, however, they were unsure of their reception, so they immediately set to work on a stockade. The redwood fort had two corner blockhouses, each housing half a dozen small cannons. Despite this martial display, an informant for Sonoma's General Mariano Vallejo reported in 1833 that "the walls could not withstand a cannon ball of any calibre," though they would certainly repel an assault with bows and arrows.

In the first few years the colonists built a commandant's house, barracks, and storehouses. They finished the Russian Orthodox chapel in 1824. (Today the restored fort is maintained by the state Department of Parks and Recreation.) Outside the stockade were cattle barns, windmills, a dairy, and two rows of houses with gardens. By the time French diplomat Duflot de Mofras visited in 1840, the fort boasted a high level of culture under its final commandant, Alexander Rotchev, and his accomplished wife, Princess Elena Gagarina. "Anyone who has led the dreary life of a trapper," wrote De Mofras, "or has been pursued by the yells of savages, can fully appreciate the joy of a choice library, French wines, a piano, and a score of Mozart." His reception, he added, was "almost European."

The Russians kept Rumiantsev (Bodega Bay) as their chief port but centered their efforts at the blufftop fort. Father Mariano Payeras, a visitor in 1822, observed a blacksmithy, forge, tannery, and bathhouse along Fort Ross Creek. The bathhouse ran on the same principle as Indian sweat houses; steam rose from hot stones sprinkled with water while the men sat on benches relaxing and swapping stories. "They enter naked and soon begin to sweat oceans," Payeras wrote in his diary.

Ross colonists began the first shipyard in California. Its singular lack of success can be blamed on the shipwrights' unfamiliarity with native wood. Chief carpenter Grudinin built four brigantines, all of improperly seasoned oak. Rot set in just as the ships were launched; within a few years not one was seaworthy. The Russians had better luck making redwood barrels, used for salting away meat and whale oil. The chief business of the outpost, however, was the sea otter hunt. The economy of Russian America was based on fur trade. A dense, glossy, otter pelt brought 40 times the price of a sable fur in the markets of Manchuria, where nobles trimmed their coats with otter fur. Ross's founding party included only 25 Russians; the rest were 80 Aleut Indians from Alaska who hunted in kayaks on the open sea. These "marine cossacks" quickly devastated local otter herds. By 1820 otters were already becoming scarce along the California coast. In 1821 the annual catch had dwindled from hundreds of pelts to only 32.

As the otters disappeared, fort managers turned to agriculture to justify Ross's existence with the Russian-American Company. Kuskov, the first manager, had a passion for gardening, planting pumpkins, squash, and watermelons. He kept Sitka, the capital of Russian America, supplied with pickled beets, and he was probably the first Sonoma County gardener to curse the persistent native gopher.

The colonists imported Sonoma County's first grapevines from Peru in 1817, and they planted hundreds of apple, cherry, and pear trees on slopes behind the fort. They also planted wheat fields near the fort, but, Payeras wrote, "These produce little, and that is of poor quality due to the extraordinary cold and constant fog."

To escape the grey weather, Russians expanded into inland valleys in the 1830s. Khlebnikov Ranch was north of the Estero de Americano, and Kostrominitov Ranch was on Willow Creek. Chernykh Rancho, which may have been near Freestone or Graton, had 2,000 vine stalks in addition to its wheat fields. The Russians were not savvy farmers, however, and never grew enough food to supply the Alaskan colonies.

The Russians hired local Kashaya Pomo to do the actual field work, and Ross became a tricultural society with Russians, Aleuts, and Pomo workers living in mutual tolerance. The Russian contingent included few women, so colonists often married Kashaya women; some of these migrated to Russia with their children when the colony folded. Unlike the Spanish, Russians had no passion for converting Indians to Christianity and showed a real interest in Indian culture. Scientist Ilia Voznesensky made detailed observations of Indian life, collecting baskets and other artifacts. Today Leningrad has the world's largest collection of Pomo and Miwok crafts.

The Russians were equally curious about nature. A Russian expedition of 1816 brought naturalists Adelbert von Chamisso and Johan Eschscholtz to the California coast; Chamisso named a frail orange flower *Eschscholtzia Californica*—the California poppy. Rotchev and Voznesensky explored the Santa Rosa plain and climbed Mount Saint Helena, naming it after the commandant's wife. But Russians weren't the only ones interested in the fertile plains in the shadow of Mount Saint Helena.

Franciscan missionaries, extending the influence of Catholic Spain, settled a strip along the California coast starting in 1769, founding missions roughly a day's journey apart. Military control was centered at four presidios: San Diego, Santa Barbara, Monterey, and San Francisco. Missions were not only churches but agricultural centers, with hundreds or thousands of Indians enlisted to work the fields, either by persuasion or by force. Each mission was supposed to last for 10 years, after which the Indians, schooled in self-sufficiency, would take over. In practice, however, Indians received little training and missions persisted as church-owned centers of entrenched wealth.

England, France, and the United States all showed interest in the Pacific Northwest, and when Russians showed up on the Sonoma coast, Spanish paranoia increased. To secure their claims to land north of the bay, the Spanish founded Mission San Rafael Arcangel (now in the town of San Rafael) in 1817. In 1821 Mexico broke away from Spain and Alta California became a territory of the new Mexican Republic.

California's Mexican Governor Don Louis Arguello was still worrying about Ross when Father Jose Altamira

asked for permission to found a new mission north of the bay. At 36, Altamira was a young go-getter, zealous and impatient with the older priests who ran Mission Dolores in San Francisco. Altamira argued that Dolores should be closed and the Indian converts relocated in a sunnier climate. Arguello and the 1823 Territorial Assembly agreed, and Altamira took a party across the bay, exploring the Petaluma, Suisun, and Napa valleys before deciding on Sonoma Valley with its "permanent springs of sweet water."

The site promised to be an agricultural paradise. "No one can doubt the mildness of the climate of Sonoma after observing the plants, the very tall trees," Altamira wrote in his diary in June 1823. On July 4, 1823, he and his party rose at dawn and blessed a temporary redwood cross. Troops fired off a volley of shots, neophytes sang hymns,

Russia and Spain were in conflict when Russia established a southern base at Fort Ross on the Sonoma coast. The Russians kept Bodega Bay as their chief port but focused their efforts on the blufftop fort, taking advantage of the coastal site. The Russian Orthodox chapel with its two towers is pictured in this photo. Courtesy, Don Silverek Photography

and Altamira celebrated mass in gratitude for the new mission, which he named New San Francisco.

Not everyone was so enthusiastic. Altamira had neglected to ask his Franciscan superiors in San Francisco for permission to trudge off into the hinterlands and start a new mission to replace their own. Altamira's elderly opponents died before they could dislodge him. As a compromise he dropped the "New" and called the Sonoma mission San Francisco Solano, in honor of a Peruvian saint. It was the last and northernmost of California's 21 missions, and the only one founded under Mexican rule.

By 1825 Altamira had a 120-foot-long adobe with a tile roof. Ironically, the Russians were good neighbors, showing up for the dedication of the church in 1824 with altar cloths, candlesticks, mirrors, and a bell. The mission, designed to thwart Russian expansion, led instead to a constant flow of trade between the two remote outposts. Russians bought wheat and cattle from the mission; missionaries came to the Russians for long boats to cross the bay.

Gradually a mission community developed with about 700 Indian residents, mostly transfers from other missions. But the Indian workers revolted against the harsh young priest; he fled to San Rafael and was replaced by Fra Buenaventura Fortuny, who was older and apparently wiser.

Altamira was not alone in being disliked. Most California Indians feared and hated the Spanish. Sonoma coast Indians like the Kashaya Pomo welcomed the Russians as a buffer against them. An anonymous ensign reporting to Mariano Vallejo in 1833 wrote that Miwok Indians around Bodega Bay watched over Russian warehouses there because the Russians in turn protected them from the Spanish. Auguste Duhaut-Cilly, a French sea captain, visited the Solano mission in August 1827 and wrote, "The Spanish government of California has always followed the atrocious system of ordering, from time to time, excursions to the settlements of the interior, either for retaking the Indians escaped from the missions, or driving away los gentiles the [non-missionized Indians] . . . expeditons which, while costing the life of some soldiers and many natives, have served but to nourish hatred."

By the 1830s the mission era was drawing to a close. Californios, the settlers from Spain, were jealous of the missions' huge land holdings. In 1833 Mexico ordered the Franciscans to emancipate the Indians and dissolve the missions. The government dispatched Mariano Guadelupe Vallejo, at age 27 the commandant of the San Francisco Presidio, to take charge of the secularization of Sonoma Mission in 1835. As commanding officer of "La Frontera del Norte" —the northern frontier—Vallejo was ordered to settle the area to assert Mexican claims and thwart the Russians.

Like many Californios who were in the right place at the right time, Vallejo benefitted immensely from the breakup of the mission system. His ranches absorbed live-

General Mariano Vallejo reviews his troops in this view of the north side of the Sonoma Plaza. This painting was made in 1880 from General Vallejo's recollection. Courtesy, California Department of Parks and Recreation and James B. Alexander

stock and Indian laborers from the San Rafael and Sonoma missions. Vallejo's mandate in the north included settlement of the region, and under his direction Sonoma County's richest land was parceled out as ranchos, chiefly to members of his own extended family, which was considerable.

Most of California's arable land was divided into 800 ranchos, most of them granted by the Mexican government between 1823 and 1846. At 66,000 acres, Vallejo's Petaluma Rancho was one of the biggest in the state. Ranchos were devoted not to crops but to cattle raised for hides; this was the colorful era of the mounted vaquero ruling vast grazing lands. Property rights were relaxed in the extreme, as noted by John Bidwell, an early American immigrant: "When you wanted a horse to ride, you would take it to the next ranch—it might be 20, 30 or 50 miles—and turn it out there, and sometime or other in reclaiming his stock the owner would get it back. In this way you might travel from one end of California to the other." A hungry traveler was allowed to kill and eat another man's cows as long as he left the hides hanging with the brand in plain sight.

The northern frontier was a wilderness; Vallejo had to persuade fellow Californios to come and apply for vast tracts of land. He convinced his widowed mother-in-law, Doña Maria Carrillo, to come north. Doña Maria packed seven Spanish trunks with her finery, assembled the nine

Carrillo children who still lived with her (three older daughters were already married), and headed north along El Camino Real to stay with her daughter Benecia, Vallejo's wife. After a brief stay in Sonoma, she moved over the hill to Santa Rosa Creek in 1837 and built the Carrillo adobe, the first European home in the Santa Rosa Valley.

Yankee sea captains, sailing between California and Peru, lived among the Californios and courted the much younger daughters of prosperous families. A handful married into the sprawling Carrillo/Vallejo family and applied for their own ranchos. Scottish sea Captain John Wilson married Benecia's sister, Ramona Carrillo, and received Los Guilucos Rancho (including present-day Kenwood) in 1837. Captain John Rogers Cooper, married to Vallejo's sister Encarnacion, took 18,000-acre El Molino Rancho (present-day Forestville) in 1836 and built the state's first power sawmill there. Captain Henry Fitch, who eloped with Benecia's sister, got the Sotoyome grant (now Healdsburg) in 1840. Fitch looked after trade in San Diego and sent Cyrus Alexander to develop the rancho, promising him 10,000 acres in return. Alexander picked the choice Alexander Valley as his payment and moved there. Merchant Jacob Leese wed Rosalia, yet another sister of Vallejo, and received the Huichica Rancho east of Sonoma.

Other ranchos went to members of the Carrillo family. In Santa Rosa Valley, Matriarch Doña Maria had the 8,800-acre Cabeza de Santa Rosa Rancho, so named because the home lay at the head (cabeza) of the creek. Her eldest son Joaquin received the 13,000-acre Llano de Santa Rosa Rancho (Sebastopol and the Laguna area); he built a home west of the Laguna and later started a hotel. British travel writer Frank Marryat, visiting the county in 1850, saw Doña Maria's son Ramon, then in his 20s, as the quintessential Californio:

Don Raymond was a striking-looking fellow, well built and muscular, with regular features, half concealed by his long black hair
and beard. The loose Spanish dress, the heavy iron spurs, the lasso hanging from the saddle, and the gaunt but fiery colt on which he was mounted, were all for work and little for show . . .

Mariano Vallejo himself built a two-story building (now preserved as the Petaluma Adobe) at his vast rancho in the Petaluma Valley. The adobe was the center of a flourishing rancho, with a tannery and blacksmith shop that turned out saddles, bridles, and spurs for Vallejo's horsemen. Indian workers filled his warehouses with corn and wheat.

But Vallejo was no mere rancher. One of the cultured power-brokers of Mexican California, he absorbed books much the way he absorbed the assets of the missions. The core of Vallejo's collection came from a German merchant who landed in 1831 with a consignment of books. The 200 volumes, some of them on the church's list of forbidden books, were in danger of being confiscated when Vallejo stepped in and acquired them for a good price.

Some ranchos went to people outside the Vallejo family. Jose Berryessa, Vallejo's sergeant, received Rancho Mallacomes (or Mayacamas), a 12,000-acre spread east of present-day Healdsburg. Swiss surveyor Jean Vioget took 23,000-acre Blucher Rancho west of present-day Sebastopol in exchange for surveying other land grants. Vioget had served under German General Blucher against Napoleon at Waterloo. William Mark West, at San Miguel Rancho between El Molino and Cabeza de Santa Rosa, was a ship's carpenter who built roofs for his neighbors' new homes.

Russia monopolized the Sonoma coast, but Vallejo persuaded three Anglo seafarers to develop a rancho just south of the Russian holdings. James Dawson, James Black, and Edward McIntosh settled the Rancho Estero Americano, named after the estuary between Marin and Sonoma counties. McIntosh built the ranch house, destined to be the focus of the strangest dispute in Sonoma County real estate.

ABOVE: *General Mariano Vallejo granted vast acreage to family and friends, including his mother-in-law, Doña Maria Carrillo, who built the Carrillo adobe in 1837. Members of the Carrillo family are pictured in this 1840 photograph. Standing are Nancy, Manuel, Albert, Eli, Mariano Avelardo, and Emma; seated in the front row are John, Marta, Benecia, Joaquin, Rosario, and, in front, Anita. Courtesy, Burton Travis Collection*

OPPOSITE, TOP: *General Mariano Vallejo was charged with attracting new settlers to Northern California during the rancho era to assert Mexican claims. He divided up vast tracts of land that were to become the backbone of California under Mexican rule. From Thompson,* Atlas of Sonoma County, California, *1877*

OPPOSITE, BOTTOM: *Cyrus Alexander earned part of the Sotoyome grant when he helped Henry Fitch, one of Mariano Vallejo's brothers-in-law, develop his rancho. Alexander took the beautiful Alexander Valley as his payment. From Thompson,* Atlas of Sonoma County, California, *1877*

McIntosh went down to Monterey alone to apply for the rancho in 1839, conveniently leaving Dawson's name off the grant application. Dawson, who signed papers with an "X" anyway, didn't discover the deception until 1843. In a rage Dawson sawed the house in two and hauled his half across the property line, applying for neighboring Rancho Pogolimi. Dawson's widow later married Frederick Blume (from which the name Bloomfield probably comes).

In 1839 the Russian-American Company added up accounts and decided the Ross colony was a lost cause. Hedged in by Mexican ranchos, the Russians could not expand the farms enough to turn a profit. Alexander Rotchev negotiated a deal in 1841 with Captain John Sutter, a powerful merchant in the Sacramento Valley. Sutter offered $30,000 for the fort's moveable assets—the proverbial lock, stock, and barrel. After a stay of 39 years on the Sonoma coast, the Russians sailed for home. The Ross colony never numbered more than 500, including about 100 Russians, but its importance was greater than its size. It marked the farthest eastward extent of Imperial Russia and spurred corresponding expansion by the Spanish and Mexicans.

Sutter sent his agent John Bidwell to Fort Ross to send along anything valuable, including, wrote Bidwell, "forty-odd pieces of old rusty cannon and one or two small

ABOVE AND FACING PAGE, BOTTOM: After withdrawal of Russian traders from Bodega Bay in 1841, Mexican and American rivalry in the region increased. In 1846 agitation for incorporation within the United States culminated in a revolt, supported by John C. Frémont, above, an American officer engaged at the time in an exploring expedition. A group of 20 settlers left Frémont's camp at Sutter's Fort on June 11, 1846. Disenchanted with Mexican rule, they mounted a rebellion known as the Bear Flag Revolt. Peter Storm, who is believed to be the creator, is shown here with the original Bear Flag. Courtesy, Napa County Historical Society; Frémont courtesy, Vacaville Heritage Council

OPPOSITE, TOP: Although the basic structure of La Casa Grande, the residence of General Mariano Vallejo, may be accurately depicted, this watercolor shows ornate detailing that probably never existed on the actual building. La Casa Grande was destroyed in an 1867 fire. Courtesy, The Bancroft Library and James B. Alexander

brass pieces, with a quantity of old French flintlock muskets, pronounced by Sutter to be of those lost by Bonaparte in 1812 in his disastrous retreat from Moscow." Bidwell spent a year at the fort, boxing up muskets and making cider from apples left behind in the Russian orchard.

With the Russians gone, the coast was clear for new settlers to move into their old haunts. German immigrants Charles Meyer and Ernest Rufus claimed the coastal strip north of the Russian River, acquiring the 18,000-acre German Rancho in 1846.

Yet another sea captain, 61-year-old Stephen Smith, took the coast south of the Russian River, settling on the

35,000-acre Bodega Rancho in 1840 with his 16-year-old Peruvian bride, Manuella Torres. The enterprising Yankee captain imported machinery for the state's first steam-powered lumber and flour mill. He also added a little culture to California, bringing three pianos around the Horn, one of which took center stage in Vallejo's parlor.

No sooner had the Russians packed up and left than a far greater invasion threatened from the east: American settlers, inspired by the accounts of mountain men like Jedediah Smith, began to trickle over the Sierras, looking for the fertile valleys of California. The first organized group was the Bartleston-Bidwell party from Missouri (the same Bidwell that John Sutter later sent to Ross). The bedraggled pioneers reached the haven of Sutter's New Helvetia settlement in 1842, followed by several hundred land-hungry settlers who moved into the Sacramento, Sonoma, and Napa valleys, much to the dismay of the Mexican government. Two Donner children, survivors of the ill-fated party trapped by Sierra snows, found a haven with settlers in Sonoma.

General Vallejo, by now one of the premier states-men of Mexican California, was tolerant of Anglos, especially with so many in his own family. Nevertheless, by 1845 Vallejo and his compatriots feared their homeland would be overrun. "The emigration of North Americans to California today forms an unbroken line of wagons from the United States clear to this Department," Vallejo wrote. "I see with regret what I predicted to the National Government more than eight years ago gradually coming true. The stream of Americans then was only considerable, and today it is frightful."

Distrust increased between Americans and Californios, fueling rumors that Mexico would expel the pioneers. In 1846 a U.S. naval contingent was poised near the port of Monterey, hoping for an excuse to annex California. American scout John C. Frémont and his band were waiting in the hills, encouraging rebellion. In June a rumor swept the pioneer community that Mexico had ordered all Americans to quit California and retrace their steps across the Sierras. In protest a party of outraged farmers, mostly from Napa and Sacramento, rode off to capture Sonoma, staging the greatest comic opera of nineteenth-century California: the Bear Flag Revolt.

Sonoma was a pueblo with few soldiers when the 33 Bear Flaggers rode up at daybreak on June 14, 1846. They were a scruffy and varied bunch as they surrounded Vallejo's Sonoma home. "Some wore the relics of their homespun garments, some relied upon the antelope and the

bear for their wardrobe," wrote one of the party. "There was the grim old hunter with his long heavy rifle, the farmer with his double-barreled shotgun . . . others with horse-pistols, revolvers, sabres, ships cutlasses, Bowie knives." Ezekiel "Stuttering" Merritt, captain of the impromptu band, and several others disappeared inside the house to talk terms with Vallejo, who generously opened up his supply of brandy. After several hours, the remaining party outside got restless and chose a captain to investigate. He did not reappear either. Finally William Ide, another of the band, slipped inside to discover the delay.

"There sat Merritt—his head fallen," wrote Ide, ". . . and there sat the new made Captain as mute as the seat he sat upon. The bottles had well nigh vanquished the captors." The Bear Flag party pulled itself together long enough to declare a revolutionary Bear Flag Republic, taking Vallejo and a few relatives hostage and hustling them off to Sutter's Fort in Sacramento, where they remained prisoners for several months. The Bears then improvised a banner "made of plain cotton cloth, and ornamented with the red flannel of a shirt from the back of one of the men," wrote Ide. The flag bore the words "California Republic" and the image of a grizzly bear, symbolizing "strength and unyielding resistence," added Ide. The Bears were not artists; onlookers reported the celebrated bear looked more like a prize porker.

The episode turned tragic when two Bears, Thomas Cowie and George Fowler, rode toward Fitch Rancho for spare ammunition. A party of Californio *defensores* waylaid the pair north of the Carrillo adobe and killed them. An avenging group of Bears, led by Frémont and Kit Carson, chased the Californio party, which escaped across the bay. Near San Rafael the Bears captured three non-combatants, Jose Berryessa and two teenaged brothers named de Haro. According to Carson's account, Frémont told Carson he "had no room for prisoners, but do your duty," whereupon Carson shot all three. The violent exchange left a legacy of bitterness between Mexicans and Yankees, an unnecessary one since many Californios, Vallejo among them, were by then resigned to the U.S. annexation.

The grizzly banner flew over Sonoma for 22 days. Word of the Mexican-American War then reached California, and the Bear revolt was absorbed into the greater conflict. The Bears had jumped the gun on history. Mexico lost the war and in 1848 ceded California to the United States. The Mexican era was at an end. Ahead were gold and statehood.

*A brass band and a crowd of citizens turned out to greet the train in this 1887
photo taken in Guerneville. Courtesy, Sonoma County Library*

Building Main Street

The 1850s were a crucial decade that saw the breakup of vast ranchos and the beginning of towns in Sonoma County. With the advent of the Mexican War, the town of Sonoma came under several years of military rule. Sonoma housed regular troops as well as Companies C and H of Stevenson's Regiment, a special unit recruited to strengthen the U.S. hold on California. Colonel Jonathan Stevenson's New York volunteers—doctors, lawyers, surveyors, mechanics—were chosen for professional skills rather than fighting ability. Some had artistic leanings. Lieutenant George Derby, writing under the name Squibob, penned humorous tales of Sonoma County life. The soldiers formed a theatrical company, enlisting their buddies to play the parts. The regiment staged bear fights, played billiards in General Vallejo's Casa de Billardo on the plaza, and livened up the town.

Mariano Vallejo himself had surveyed Sonoma in the 1830s, laying out a large town square surrounded by lots. By the late 1840s Sonoma's square was an animated but neglected place. Enterprising workmen dug up adobe for bricks and left yawning holes. In one spot a ditch ran through the plaza with a cannon wheel over it as a makeshift bridge. Stevenson's boys and their Californio friends took turns breaking wild horses in the square, in between cockfights and horse races.

The military occupation brought to Sonoma officers like Joseph Hooker and William T. Sherman, who would later distinguish themselves in the Civil War. A veteran of Mexican campaigns, Hooker bought 500 acres in the Valley of the Moon with visions of being a country squire, but when the Civil War broke out he headed east. Wangling an appointment with President Lincoln, Hooker modestly told him, "I was at Bull Run the other day, Mr. President, and it is no vanity in me to say that I am a damned sight better general than any you had on that field." Despite his egotism, Hooker became a favorite of Lincoln's; the president eventually promoted him to commander of the Army of the Potomac.

In February 1848 John Sutter wrote to Vallejo of a gold discovery in the Sierra foothills. Two weeks later Sutter was paying off his debts in Sonoma with samples of gold dust. The gold rush, which brought 100,000 newcomers to California, had the opposite effect on Sonoma.

Within weeks the town was practically empty. A French consul on the scene wrote of Sonoma: "Most of its houses are empty, all work has stopped, and there as everywhere else, there is not a single carpenter left nor a joiner, nor a blacksmith nor any laborer doing the least work. All have gone to the Placer, or have come back from there too rich and too independent to resume their trades . . ."

Townsmen and soldiers alike left Sonoma for the hills. Surveyor Jasper O'Farrell put down his compass and headed for gold country with Jacob Leese, coming home with a tidy profit. Stevenson's boys forgot their regimental duties and followed close behind. Storeowners like Lilburn Boggs did a brisk trade supplying miners until boats took miners directly up the Sacramento River, bypassing Sonoma. The gold rush was in full swing by 1849, giving its name to the 49ers who hastened to California by three routes. Some sailed 18,000 miles around Cape Horn; others shipped to Panama, crossed the isthmus, and came up the coast by paddle-wheel steamer. The majority, especially those from the Ohio and Mississippi valleys, came overland on the California Trail in mile-long wagon trains.

Some who left Sonoma limped back with empty pockets; others returned with fortunes in gold. Helpers at the Blue Wing, a popular tavern and gambling hall, supplemented their income sweeping gold dust off the barroom floor. Dozens of Stevenson's men got discharges and came back to Sonoma, where their qualifications for the regiment also made them admirable townsfolk. Captain John Frisbie, once the commander of H Company, came home to marry one of Vallejo's daughters and open a store in his father-in-law's Casa Grande. A.J. Cox started the county's first newspaper, the *Sonoma Bulletin*, in 1852. C Company's Captain John Brackett represented Sonoma in the first legislature that convened after California became a state in 1850.

Not everyone came to California for gold. Baron Agostin Haraszthy, a Hungarian aristocrat, saw Sonoma Valley as the perfect setting for wine grapes. Political turmoil in Europe drove him to America in 1840, where he pursued a varied career—farming in Wisconsin, publishing tales of his travels, and finally trekking west on the Santa Fe Trail. His California career was equally diverse: he was sheriff in San Diego and later an official of the San

Francisco mint. Vallejo invited Haraszthy to Sonoma in 1856, where he recognized an untapped potential for grapes. "The production is fabulous," Haraszthy wrote in *Grape Culture, Wine and Wine-Making*, "and there is no doubt in my mind that before long there will be localities discovered which will furnish as noble wines as Hungary, Spain, France, or Germany ever have produced." After Haraszthy proved grapes could prosper without irrigation, he went on a state-sponsored tour of Europe in 1861, returning with 300 varieties that became the foundation of Sonoma County's vast wine industry. He planted 6,000 acres of vineyards and founded the Buena Vista Viticultural Socety. Jacob Gundlach and other Sonoma growers came to him for cuttings, and so did vintners from other parts of the state, creating, says local historian Ernest Finley, a "grape rush." Haraszthy and Vallejo competed for wine ribbons at the state fair, but the rivalry was a friendly one: in 1863 Haraszthy's sons Arpad and Attila married Vallejo's daughters Natalie and Jovita. Setbacks in the 1860s prompted Haraszthy to pursue business ventures in Central America, where his death was as colorful as his life. The father of Sonoma County winemaking lost his life crossing a river in Nicaragua; some accounts conclude he was devoured by a alligator.

Meanwhile, the gold rush sparked a town in southern Sonoma County. In 1849, 40,000 new people surged into a state unprepared to feed them; by 1852, 60,000

more had followed. The Petaluma Valley was a paradise of game that drew hunters up the winding Petaluma River. Hunting was a lucrative profession: deer fetched $20 a head in San Francisco markets; quail were $9 a dozen. Two hunters, Tom Baylis and Dave Flogsdel, each put up a trading post at the upper reaches of the river. Baylis later built a warehouse and the Pioneer Hotel, running his own sloop to and from San Francisco. James Hudspeth opened a warehouse at the foot of Washington Street when he discovered he could ship Bodega potatoes cheaper from Petaluma than from Bodega Bay. Meat, wheat, and produce flowed from Sonoma County valleys to the Petaluma wharf, going by boat across the bay to San Francisco or up the Sacramento River. The steamer *Petaluma* embarked on its shake-down cruise in October 1857, chugging down the creek and across to Benecia. The *Sonoma Democrat* reported "some little roughness in her machinery, incident to all new engines," but otherwise it was a successful maiden voyage.

By 1852 the town was taking shape. Mail came on horseback once a week from Benecia. Garrett Keller claimed 158 acres of future downtown Petaluma, and

In 1849 James Cooper and Thomas Spriggs, the latter a ship's carpenter, enlarged this old Sonoma building to its present form and began operating it as a combined hotel, restaurant, and casino. Known as the Blue Wing Hotel, it was a popular gathering place for many early Californians. Courtesy, James B. Alexander

though his legal title was in doubt, buyers confidently purchased the $10 lots and Petaluma grew quickly. In 1855 there were 481 voters; the next year 801. Petaluma's first newspaper, the *Sonoma County Journal*, began in 1855; the *Argus* closely followed and the two merged in the 1860s. Between 1854 and 1860 Petaluma grew faster than any other town in the county, outstripping Sonoma. "The place already contains 2,500 inhabitants, and the air of business and prosperity which it wears is quite striking," wrote New York reporter Bayard Taylor in 1859. Petaluma did not, however, get the coveted status of county seat, an honor which went instead to Santa Rosa.

The nucleus of early activity in Santa Rosa Valley was Doña Maria Carrillo's adobe ranchhouse. David Mallagh, husband of Doña Maria's daughter Juana, and his partner Donald McDonald ran a hotel and store there for traders taking freight by mule to Clear Lake and the Russian River. In 1852 they sold the business to Alonzo Meacham, who in turn sold out to Feodor Hahman, Berthold "Barney" Hoen, and William Hartman, three Germans destined to be movers and shakers in the valley. Soon Hoen and company also bought 70 acres of future downtown Santa Rosa for $1,600 and surveyed the land for a town. Lots went for $25 each. Julio Carrillo's house was the first in the area, built a year before the survey. The first streets bore number and letter names, but later developers didn't follow this simple scheme. The most colorful sequence of street names is described by turn-of-the-century historian Tom Gregory: "An addition was attached to the city by a Mr. Pipher, who had learned to play football at Palo Alto, and the streets of the tract bore the academic legend 'Leland-Stanford-Junior-University,' names fully as unique and as inappropriate for the purpose as would be 'In-God-We-Trust-All-Others-Cash.'"

Franklin Town, on the north bank of Santa Rosa Creek, was an early rival of Santa Rosa. French-Canadian Oliver Beaulieu (variously spelled Bolio, Boileau, etc.) surveyed the town in 1853; John Ball built a small hotel and store there. Franklin's Baptist Church was the first church

The rivalry between Sonoma and fledgling Santa Rosa for the county seat was a hot issue during the state assembly elections of 1853. In September 1854, 716 voted for Santa Rosa as opposed to 563 for Sonoma, thus securing Santa Rosa as county seat. Pictured here is the courthouse in Santa Rosa as it appeared around 1895. Courtesy, Don Silverek Photography

in the valley. The creekside town was Santa Rosa's twin until the celebrated caper of the county seat.

Sonoma, being the only town in the district, was named county seat when the legislature established counties after statehood in 1850. (Sonoma County also included present-day Mendocino County until 1859.) Rivalry between Sonoma and fledgling Santa Rosa was a hot issue in 1854, when State Assemblyman James Bennett of Santa Rosa introduced a bill to let Sonoma County voters choose their county seat. Santa Rosa boosters Barney Hoen and Julio Carrillo pledged to donate land for a new courthouse. Even the *Sonoma Bulletin* admitted the Sonoma courthouse had its failings, noting that officials ran "the risk of being crushed beneath a mass of mud and shingles, for we really believe it will cave in the next heavy rain."

To impress voters with the splendor of Santa Rosa, town fathers held a Fourth of July barbecue and fed everyone within voting distance—about 500 citizens. The shindig had the desired effect: In September 1854, 716

ABOVE AND LEFT: By the time A.W. Russell launched Santa Rosa's first newspaper, the Sonoma Democrat, *on October 22, 1857, Santa Rosa had grown to 100 buildings. By the end of the decade it had 400 citizens and a host of thriving businesses fronting the plaza. Courtesy, Don Silverek Photography*

voted for Santa Rosa versus 563 for Sonoma. Santa Rosans feared Sonomans would not lightly surrender their court records. Slow-moving bureaucracy was not the Santa Rosa style in those days. Following the vote Jim Williamson hitched two mules to a wagon and in the company of county clerk N. M. Menefee rode into Sonoma, loaded up the dusty documents and took off for Santa Rosa 22 miles away. The one-legged Menefee sat beside Williamson, occasionally prodding one of the mules with the end of his peg leg. In this fashion the county records entered the new county seat full tilt. Williamson's charge for the 100-minute freight run was $15.

After the hijacking, A.J. Cox, the wry voice of the *Sonoma Bulletin,* remarked,

We are only sorry they did not take the adobe courthouse along—not because it would be an ornament to Santa Rosa, but because its removal would have embellished our plaza.

Alas 'old casa de adobe.' No more do we see county lawyers and loafers in general, lazily engaged in the laudable effort of whittling asunder the veranda posts—which, by the way, require but little more cutting to bring the whole dilapidated fabric to the ground.

Santa Rosa's elevation to county seat was the death knell for nearby Franklin Town. John Ball and his neighbors moved the mile and a half down the creek to the new town, never dreaming twentieth-century Santa Rosa would expand to include their old haunts.

By the time A.W. Russell launched Santa Rosa's first newspaper, the *Sonoma Democrat*, on October 22, 1857, Santa Rosa had grown to 100 buildings. By the end of the decade it had 400 citizens and a host of thriving businesses fronting the plaza. Williamson's California Livery Stable competed with the Union Livery Stable, once owned by Julio Carrillo. Santa Rosa Bakery sold loaves three for a quarter. Jason Miller's ad for his dry goods store boasted it was in "the fire-proof brick store" in the plaza's southwest corner, a sign that wooden buildings stood in jeopardy from sudden fires. On the opposite corner Henry Moller's Liquor and Oyster Saloon served fresh oysters all night. The Santa Rosa Shaving Saloon handled laundry and baths (10 baths for $4). The Eureka Hotel boasted a bar and billiards, and E.P. Colgan's Santa Rosa House offered stage connections to Petaluma, the Russian River, Sonoma, and the Geysers.

Farther north on the road to Mendocino, Harmon Heald settled on the Sotoyome Rancho in 1850 and claimed land for a town site. Heald surveyed the town in 1857 and sold lots for $15 apiece, setting aside parcels for a school, cemetery, plaza, and churches. By the end of the decade Healdsburg had 500 people and 120 houses. Satirist A. J. Cox had folded his *Sonoma Bulletin* in 1855, announcing to his loyal readers that "the Blunderbuss has dried up." In 1860, however, he turned up as editor of the fledgling *Review,* one of several papers destined to cover Healdsburg news.

More towns emerged farther north. Colonel A.C. Godwin started a store in 1854 that was the nucleus of Geyserville. R.B. Markle bought 800 acres of land near the present Mendocino border. Levi Rosenberg and the Hahman/Hartman team opened stores, while Markle ran a tavern for thirsty pack-train drivers. This stop evolved into

Healdsburg owes its beginnings to Harmon G. Heald, who settled part of the Sotoyome Rancho in 1850. Heald platted the townsite in 1857, including areas designated for a school, churches, a plaza, and a cemetery. By 1860 Healdsburg boasted 120 homes and 500 residents. From Thompson, Atlas of Sonoma County, California, *1887*

Cloverdale. Windsor also started in the mid-1850s with a store and public house; a district of the present town bore the unfortunate name Poor Man's Flat. West county mill towns—Guerneville, Cazadero, Duncans Mills—trace their roots to these early times but did not come into their own until the coming of the railroads.

Joaquin Carrillo was the first Sebastopol resident, building his adobe house on his Llano de Santa Rosa Rancho in 1846. Around the same time James Miller and John Walker founded a store a mile south of the present town. J.H.P. Morris started a rival grocery and saloon, calling his center Pine Grove. Surveyor Jasper O'Farrel named the district Analy (for his sister Ann) when townships were established in the 1860s, but a fistfight in 1856 provided the lasting name for the town. Hibbs, one of the combatants, had retreated into Dougherty's store in Pine Grove. Hibbs wouldn't come out and Dougherty prevented his attackers from coming in. Onlookers compared this local battle to the siege of Sebastopol then going on in the Crimean War.

When California became a territory of the United States, land-hungry pioneers poured in to stake out homesteads in the Golden State's fertile valleys. Gold fever drew thousands more farmers who scouted around for land when their get-rich schemes fell through. Most found themselves in a prolonged legal limbo in which they could neither buy land nor verify who really owned it.

The Treaty of Guadalupe Hidalgo, ending the Mexican-American War in 1848, upheld the property rights of former Mexican citizens. In 1851 the U.S. Congress set up a land commission to verify California land claims. Rancho owners hunted through forgotten trunks for documents proving the boundaries of their land. The commission rejected nearly 200 claims, which then were open to homesteaders. Over 600 claims were confirmed, but only after lengthy appeals by government attorneys. It took an average of 17 years to confirm a land grant; most owners had to break up their huge holdings because they were bankrupt when they finally established title. Mariano Vallejo, for instance, received 44,000 acres of his original 66,000-acre claim, but the financial strain forced him to sell his Petaluma adobe and surrounding land to settlers.

The commission threw out some imaginative claims. Jose Yves Limantour, a French merchant working in Mexico, claimed Sonoma's mission vineyards as well as half of San Francisco and the islands of Alcatraz, Yerba Buena, and the Farallones. U.S. attorneys claimed the signature on Limantour's grant was not that of the Mexican governor, though it did resemble the handwriting of Limantour's secretary. Limantour reaped a quarter of a million dollars from gullible buyers before the federal government threw out his claim. By then he had taken his movable assets back to Mexico.

American farmers, accustomed to homesteading on open land, were dismayed to find all the best land already claimed. Most farmers squatted, hoping the land would become public if the claim were rejected. No one wanted to make improvements to land belonging to someone else, so the first homes were makeshift shanties made of posts and split redwood. In the 1850s these "bachelor ranchos"

Although Paul Hahman's Santa Rosa apothecary business was destroyed in the 1906 earthquake, his ledger shows business as usual resumed just two days later. The drugstore, which is shown as it looked in 1890, had the first plate glass window in Santa Rosa's new downtown. Courtesy, Sonoma County Library

gave way to established farms as families moved in. Settlers clustered at Green Valley, Bodega, Santa Rosa Creek, Dry Creek, and the Russian River Valley, hoping Mexican grants would be tossed out.

In many ways Eliza and James Gregson were typical of these early pioneers. In their early 20s the Gregsons left Illinois with Eliza's mother and two brothers and crossed the plains with ox teams. The exhausted party arrived at Sutter's Fort in 1846, where James worked as a blacksmith and also helped guard the Vallejo party during the Bear Flag Revolt. The Gregsons were the first to settle in Green Valley near Sebastopol, squatting on a 160-parcel they later purchased.

A pioneer with the instincts of a historian, Eliza Gregson wrote her memoirs on the backs of old letters, leaving a rare account of daily life around 1850. She describes tending survivors of the Donner party and seeing glimpses of the first gold dust from Sutter's Mill. She recalls (without much punctuation) the valley when it was virgin land: "when we came to green valley it seemed almost like a paradise . . . grass and clover and flowers in abundance the grass was as tall as myself." Eliza was a witness to the settlement of valleys and the founding of towns like Healdsburg and Sebastopol, while farmers organized county fairs and built better houses, "Leaveing old cabbins to be used for outhouses."

By the time rancho owners proved their claims, dozens of squatters had put down roots. Some formed Squatters Leagues and fought eviction, especially when rancho owners refused to lease or sell. There was bloodshed in Sacramento and Santa Clara, and in Sonoma County skirmishes erupted on the Bodega and Sotoyome ranchos.

Stephen Smith, claimant of the Bodega Rancho, died in 1855; Tyler Curtis married his widow in 1856 and took over the rancho. Smith was easy-going about squatters, but the hard-nosed Curtis obtained a writ of eviction in 1859. The settlers refused to budge, arguing (wrongly) that their farms were not included in the grant boundary. Curtis went down to San Francisco and hired 50 bouncers

This Santa Rosa Saloon photo was taken at the turn of the century. The rear tables were for cards and light meals. Courtesy, Sonoma County Museum

to help in the eviction; his party landed at Petaluma wharf and marched toward Bodega. The squatters got wind of the invasion and 300 of them gathered with rifles to confront Curtis. Finding himself outnumbered, Curtis suddenly expressed a willingness to rent the land at bargain prices. The settlers then marched Curtis' army back to the Petaluma docks, ending the bloodless "Bodega War."

The Sotoyome affair ended less happily. Josephine Bailhache, daughter of Henry Fitch, proved her title to the Sotoyome Rancho around Healdsburg in 1858 and spent several years hassling with entrenched squatters. Local sentiment for squatters ran high, so in 1862 Sheriff J.M. Bowles sent all the way to Petaluma for militia to evict Alexander Skaggs and other settlers. A few months later Bailhache's workman Robert Ferguson was fatally shot while dismantling squatter fences. A.L. Norton, Bailhache's attorney and agent, retaliated by burning out Sotoyome squatters. "Some of the houses were good two-story buildings," Norton later wrote, "but I treated them as I would have done a lot of rats' nests . . . The squatters continued to hang around like the French soldiers around a burning Moscow until the elements drove them away to the hills, where some of them put up temporary adobes on the adjacent government land."

The scrappy Norton, a veteran of skirmishes over gold rush claims, made a profession out of evicting squatters from ranchos. He left the goldfields for a law practice in Placerville. When Placerville was gutted by fire in 1856, Norton moved down to Healdsburg and soon became the terror of local squatters.

The consistent losers in the land wars were the Indians, who were dispossessed of their native lands. A majority had already died from smallpox, cholera, and measles brought by whites. In 1837 a Mexican corporal from Sonoma contracted smallpox at Fort Ross and the disease spread inland. Whole villages in the Sonoma, Napa, and Suisin areas were wiped out. Julio Carrillo later told of seeing the bones of hundreds of Indian victims of the disease. Survivors watched settlers turn their ancestral lands into farms. Some found seasonal work in the fields. *Harper's Magazine* in 1861 chronicled the maltreatment of California Indians, reporting, "Of those that failed to perish from hunger or exposure, some were killed on the general prin-

ciple that they must have subsisted by stealing cattle." In 1853 the federal government set aside small reservations, but the *Petaluma Journal* of April 15, 1857, reported whites had killed 300 Indians near the Round Valley reservaton in Mendocino, in retaliation for Indians eating their cattle. Starvation, disease, murder, and kidnapping further reduced the numbers of native Americans, although isolated groups like the Kashaya Pomo near Stewart's Point maintained their traditions.

On May 25, 1861, the Pony Express brought the

OPPOSITE: These Santa Rosa High School ninth grade students posed for this photo in 1892. Courtesy, Sonoma County Museum

BELOW: As more families settled in Sonoma County, the need to educate and develop the children grew. Schools became the focal point in rural communities, and teachers were highly respected members of the community. Pictured here is the Kenwood School in the 1890s. Courtesy, Don Silverek Photography

news of the Confederate attack on Fort Sumter. The *Petaluma Journal* rushed out a special 8 p.m. edition on the start of the Civil War. California had entered the Union only 10 years previously as a free state, but Southern sympathy ran high in pockets, especially in Sonoma County, which had a high percentage of settlers with Confederate ties. In 1850 approximately one-quarter of Sonoma County's 562 residents (not counting Indians) were born in Missouri, Kentucky, Tennessee, or Virginia. An exception was Petaluma, initially settled by Yankee traders and foreign merchants. Californians were subject to Federal draft, but eastern Yankees didn't call upon their west coast brethren to fight, chiefly because of the cost of shuttling troops 3,000 miles to the battlefield. Relegated to the status of onlookers, Sonoma County partisans drew their own Mason-Dixon Line somewhere between Petaluma and Santa Rosa and waged war in the pages of rival newspapers.

Chief combatants were Samuel Cassiday, editor of the *Petaluma Argus,* and Thomas L. Thompson, editor of Santa Rosa's *Democrat.* Cassiday, raised in Ohio, tried his hand at dairy farming, mining, and teaching before turning to journalism as a supporter of Lincoln's Republican party and critic of the Southern "Copperheads." Thompson was a Virginian who started his newspaper career at age 12 in the office of the *West Virginian* before coming west. He started the *Petlauma Journal* at age 17, selling it in 1856 and buying Santa Rosa's *Sonoma Democrat* in 1860. Friends described him as "a man of great information, genial in his manners," but the words flung across the county between the *Democrat* and the *Argus* were anything but genial.

The *Democrat* blasted Lincoln's "unwise, unholy and fratricidal war," and railed against the anti-slavery movement and the "pretended amelioration of the African race" (September 4, 1862).

Lincoln's Emancipation Proclamation freeing the slaves had Thompson frothing, "By a mere stroke of the pen wielded in the hand of his Highness, Abraham Lincoln, three millions of Negro slaves, the property of the citizens of the United States, were declared forever free . . ." (January 3, 1863).

Cassiday charged that someone at the *Democrat,*

ABOVE: An early REO truck loaded with sacks of hops at the Wood Ranch in Fulton portrays the fruitful harvest that hard work and rich Sonoma County soil could yield. Courtesy, Sonoma County Museum

OPPOSITE: Wild oats and hay covered the hills and valleys of this fertile countryside long before the first settlers moved into the area. Early work crews would move throughout the countryside, cutting and baling hay for the local settlers or for shipping. They would set up camp and work from dawn to dusk until they finished. Courtesy, Don Silverek Photography

"malignant in his hatred to our Government, has taken possession of its columns" (April 7, 1864). The following week Thompson blasted the *Argus'* use of "low personalities and epithets which are the usual weapons of fools."

In Petaluma, the skirmish over the bell in the Petaluma Baptist Church was a microcosm of the Civil War. Manville "Matt" Doyle rescued the bell from a San Francisco junkyard in 1856, and it served as a town bell, tolling for emergencies as well as Sunday service. During the war, pro-Lincoln parishioners rang the bell for Union victories too, until churchgoers didn't know whether to put on their Sunday clothes, run out to fight a fire, or cheer for the Union. Doyle, a Southern sympathizer, was especially incensed since he helped buy the bell in the first place. Finally Doyle and friends came out with a block and tackle and liberated the bell, hiding it under potato sacks in a riverside warehouse. Then they nailed up the church for good measure. The next day Union Baptists rescued the bell and carted it back to church on a wagon draped with the American flag. They hoisted it back into the steeple and rang it loud and long, celebrating their victory but also cracking the bell. (Others say the bell cracked when it rang out the news of Lincoln's assassination. The bell, crack and all, is now on display at the Pioneer

Museum in San Francisco.)

Editorial warfare reached new lows after the 1864 election, when Lincoln took every California county except Sonoma. "Sonoma County has to stand as the Judas among the Brethren, as the black spot, and only spot on the coast where Treason has polled a large majority of votes," Cassiday wrote. He was gratified that Petaluma and Bloomfield went for Lincoln. "But there are other precincts where the people are of the lowest type of the Gorilla tribe, wild and uncultivated savages, from the wilds of Arkansas, Missouri, Texas, etc., who can neither read nor write, nor think" (November 11, 1864). Thompson countered, ". . . we of Sonoma county have the happy reflection that those who may live in after years to regret the triumph of despotism in free America, cannot say that we did it."

The South capitulated in the spring of 1865, and the venomous exchanges subsided. When John Wilkes Booth assassinated Lincoln on April 14, 1865, Thompson issued an edition, heavily lined in black, out of respect—and fear. San Franciscans, outraged at the president's murder, sacked the offices of five Secessionist papers in the city. In Petaluma, the boys of Hueston's Guard saddled up with vague intentions of riding north and doing the same to the *Democrat*. Local lore says the marauders rode as far north as the Washoe House tavern, where the excellent beer distracted them and put an end to the invasion of Santa Rosa.

With the war over, Petalumans, Santa Rosans, and their neighbors returned to their customary preoccupations: raising cows, chickens, grapes, hops, and apples—and getting them all to market. The area was on the threshold of tremendous expansion. The coming of the railroad would transform Sonoma County from a quiet rural enclave into a major supplier of produce to the world.

Cycling became a popular sport in Sonoma County soon after the Civil War, when the velocipede, or three-wheeler, was the favored cycle. By the 1890s the two-wheeler with a large front wheel became the cycle of choice. The Empire Wheelmen, organized in 1880, promoted cycling with ambitious trips such as a two-week jaunt to Yosemite and back. The Wheelmen leased a clubhouse that still stands on Cherry Street in Santa Rosa, and met for noon lunches, cards, and billiards. Courtesy, Sonoma County Museum

CHAPTER FOUR

Commerce in Motion

Railroads came to Sonoma County in the 1870s. Steam locomotives quickened the pulse of commerce and boosted trade with the Port of San Francisco, providing world-wide markets for timber, eggs, grapes, hops, and produce. Nothing in Sonoma County's history changed the area so fast as the railroads. Maritime transport was crucial, too. Schooners cruised the North Coast to pick up timber; steamboats on the estuaries provided the vital link between San Francisco and rail lines that ended at Petaluma, Sausalito, and San Rafael.

In the two decades before the advent of rail lines, however, stages and ox-carts hauled passengers and freight. In summer, stagecoach passengers covered their faces with bandanas to keep out clouds of dust. In the winter drivers coaxed their teams along highways that turned into rivers of mud. The driver's job was prestigious but rugged; passengers had a rough time of it, too. The stage from Santa Rosa, for instance, was traveling downhill toward Petaluma one rainy spring day in 1864 when the coach hit a stump and threw the driver from his seat. "The horses ran a short distance and turned into a narrow by-lane, where they soon fetched up against a fence," the *Petaluma Argus* reported. "The passengers . . . did not stand on the order of their going, but emptied themselves out of the stage in a hurry." A blinding rain was blamed for the mishap.

Stages pulled by teams of six horses made daily trips up the central highway that ran north from Petaluma through Santa Rosa, Windsor, Healdsburg, Geyserville, and Cloverdale. Another major thoroughfare went from Petaluma through Bloomfield, Valley Ford, Bodega Corners, Bodega Bay, and on up the coast through Fort Ross to Gualala. One of the county's oldest roads went from Petaluma to Sonoma and up the valley through Glen Ellen to Santa Rosa. Another began at Petaluma and went north through Sebastopol to Green Valley.

Where stages run there will naturally be stage robbers—or "footpads," as unmounted robbers were called. Determined bandits strung a rope across the road near Green Valley and halted the Miller and Co. stage from Santa Rosa to Bodega in December 1871, escaping with $286 from the Wells Fargo box.

Wells Fargo's nemesis was Black Bart, a notoriously genteel bandit who plagued the company up and down the state between 1875 and 1883. The lone bandit pulled 28 robberies—several in Sonoma and Mendocino counties—always with the same modus operandi. A lone man on foot disguised by a flour sack mask appeared on the road, pointed his double-barrel shotgun at the driver, and demanded the Wells Fargo box and U.S. mail. After his fourth robbery—the first in Sonoma County—the previously unnamed robber left behind an empty cash box, a poem, and his nickname.

Coast rancher George W. Call was riding south to catch the Duncans Mills train to San Francisco on August 3, 1877, when he came upon a man drinking from a stream three miles below Fort Ross. The fellow jumped up and asked if the stage had gone by. Call said the stage would be along soon and continued on his way. The man hurried on to Shotgun Point, robbed the stage, and left a tantalizing note in the otherwise empty express box: "I've labored long and hard for bread, for honor and for riches, but on my corns too long you've tred, you fine-haired sons of bitches." The verse was signed "Black Bart, the PO8."

The persistent bandit robbed the same stage in 1880 and held up the Cloverdale stage in 1882 and 1883. Bart's luck ran out in 1883 when he left behind a handkerchief during a botched holdup. Wells Fargo detective J.B. Hume traced the kerchief's laundry mark to a San Francisco laundry and arrested C.E. Boles, alias Charles Bolton, who was posing as a distinguished, middle-aged mining engineer. Boles was released after four years in San Quentin and promised to go straight. The warden asked if he planned to write any more poetry. Boles replied, "I've just told you, warden, I promise to commit no more crimes." Then he vanished. Rumors persisted that Wells Fargo paid him a stipend to refrain from robbing their stages.

The most celebrated stage rides went to the Geysers in the hills northeast of Healdsburg. William Elliott, tracking a bear, was the first white settler to come upon the geothermal fields; they soon became a renowned tourist spectacle as famous in their day as Yosemite is now. Historian J.P. Munro-Fraser wrote in 1880, "Of all the noted places in Sonoma county, indeed on the Pacific coast, the most famous is the Geysers . . . It is positively a most 'uncanny' place." All the county's major hotels advertised stage trips to the Geysers. Roads were built from Healds-

ABOVE: The stagecoach, a buckboard, and some locals paused for this captured 1875 moment in front of the John Folks Hotel. Courtesy, Sonoma County
Library

OPPOSITE, TOP: Giant trees like this one were felled throughout the Redwood Empire during the early days of the lumber industry. Courtesy, Don Silverek Photography

OPPOSITE, BOTTOM: Vast redwood forests attracted lumbermen to the county as the demand for construction materials rose with the population. This
1880s shot, taken in the redwoods at Guerneville on the Russian River, seems
to indicate a gathering of labor and management, or perhaps a group of sightseers posing in front of the felled redwood trunk. Courtesy, Sonoma County
Museum

burg and Cloverdale, and Colonel A.G. Godwin put up the
two-story Geysers Hotel with a veranda overlooking
sulphurous Pluton Canyon. Journalist Bayard Taylor,
whose writings publicized the Geysers, visited in 1862.
"The rocks burn under you," he wrote. "You are enveloped
in fierce heat, strangled by puffs of diabolical vapor, and
stunned by the awful, hissing, spitting, sputtering, roaring,
threatening sounds—as if a dozen steamboats blowing
through their escape-pipes, had aroused the ire of ten-
thousand hell-cats."

No less famous was the hair-raising ride to the Geysers, especially in the hands of driver Clark Foss, who
made a handy living escorting parties there. Foss was
legendary for his bravado and casual disregard of
precipices as he raced along. The heart-stopping trip over
the hills was the stagecoach version of a roller coaster ride.
Robert Louis Stevenson, commenting on Foss' cult standing, wrote, "Along the unfenced, abominable mountain
roads, he launches his team with small regard to human
life or the doctrine of probabilities. Flinching travellers,
who behold themselves coasting eternity at every corner,
look with natural admiration at their driver's huge, impas-
sive, fleshy countenance."

Ships provided the only reliable transport for isolated communities along the rocky Sonoma coast.
Commerce increased dramatically in the 1850s when the
demand for lumber rose and mills sprang up to meet it. A
handful of Northern California ports—Mendocino, Noyo,
Humboldt, and Crescent City—could accommodate large
boats. The rest had anchorage only for "dog-hole"

schooners, so-called because they could weigh anchor in a spot just big enough for a dog to turn around in. Every little cove along the Sonoma coast was a dog-hole port where schooners called regularly for timber, split wood, and tanbark oak used in the tanning process. Schooners with crews of half a dozen would stay offshore, loading and unloading goods with a sliding chute that hung out over the water. Railroad ties, cordwood, and even passengers would come flying down the chute while a deck hand caught them at the other end. The major commodity was lumber from mills at Fort Ross, Salt Point, Helmke's Mill, Fisk's Landing, and mills on the Gualala River. In the 1870s the largest mill on the Sonoma coast was Duncans Mill, producing 25,000 feet of lumber per day. The Duncan brothers, Samuel and Alexander, had a mill at Salt Point; they relocated near the mouth of the Russian River and in the late 1870s moved again farther upstream (to present-day Duncans Mills)

near the new railroad.

Redwood was a favorite material for construction. Douglas fir, available on the coast in great quantities, was among the finest materials for ship building. From the 1850s to the 1920s, the West Coast was the world center of wooden ship building.

The jagged coastline with its hidden reefs and sudden winter storms claimed more than its share of ships.

ABOVE: *Petaluma's prosperity was due chiefly to its river commerce. The Steamer Gold Line, with a connection to the Petaluma and Santa Rosa Railroad, operated the* Gold, *which carried passengers, and the* Petaluma, *a freight boat. They churned back and forth between Petaluma and the San Francisco waterfront. Pictured here is the passenger steamer* Gold. *Courtesy, Don Silverek Photography*

OPPOSITE: *The dairy industry was another prominent enterprise in Petaluma. This dairy farm was photographed sometime around 1880. Courtesy, Don Silverek Photography*

RIGHT: *Bodega Creamery seems to be experiencing an early morning rush to pick up fresh cream for delivery. Bodega Creamery sits in the heart of the dairyland in Sonoma County. Some areas such as this have changed very little throughout the years. Cattle can still be seen grazing on the coastal hills and houses and buildings have remained intact and well maintained. Courtesy, Sonoma County Museum*

The *Abraham Lincoln,* owned by rancher A. Richardson of Stewart's Point, was carrying 75,000 feet of lumber when it was battered against the cliffs at Stewart's Point in 1875. Two vessels were wrecked on the same night in 1854 at the Fish Rocks just north of Gualala; one was the steamer *Arispa,* which hit the reef in rough seas. The captain drained his cargo of liquor and jerryrigged a life raft out of empty barrels. One passenger reported "he never saw as many woe-begone visages on one occasion as there were on the deck of the Arispa when the sparkling liquor gurgled from the bung-holes and passed out through the scuppers into the ocean."

One of the later wrecks was the *Pomona,* steaming

north toward Eureka on St. Patrick's Day in 1908 when it struck a sunken reef two miles south of Fort Ross. The Call family, coming down from their Fort Ross ranch, helped the 84 passengers get safely to shore.

In southern Sonoma County, estuaries linking Sonoma and Petaluma to San Pablo Bay were ready-made avenues for commerce. Boats on these tidal creeks provided a regular and cheap mode of transport to San Francisco. Traffic on the Petaluma estuary began in earnest in the 1850s when Charles Minturn, the bay's "Ferryboat King," instituted service to Lakeview six miles downstream from Petaluma. Packet boats and schooners skimmed over mudflats all the way to Petaluma, and eventually the creek was dredged so the biggger steamers could get through. Stage lines and later the Petaluma and Santa Rosa Railroad funneled people and freight to the Petaluma docks for passage to San Francisco. River commerce was a major factor in the town's prosperity. Steamers, scow schooners, and barges carried wool, butter, cream, eggs, live chicks, and incubators down the twisting tidal river to the bay. By the turn of the century the Petaluma River was the third busiest waterway in the state, after the Sacramento and the San Joaquin.

Steamers, introduced to California during the gold rush, went down the San Joaquin or all the way up the Sacramento River to Red Bluff. The Steamer Gold Line, with a connection to the Petaluma and Santa Rosa Railroad, operated the *Gold,* which carried passengers, and the *Petaluma,* a freight

boat that churned back and forth between Petaluma and the San Francisco waterfront. *Petaluma #1* was built in 1857 and was destroyed in 1900. *Petaluma #2* caught fire at the Petaluma wharf in 1914 and burned to the waterline with a full cargo; the crew had to push the boat out into the river to save the wharf. Its engines were saved and installed in its successor, *Petaluma #3.*

The first *Gold* was just as unlucky. It was fully loaded and tied up at the Petaluma docks when a midnight fire broke out onboard. A strong wind pinned it against the dock, so that boat, wharf, and warehouse all went up in flames.

Petaluma #3 had a round bow and a scow-like bottom. It was a plain, work-horse boat, designed expressly for the Petaluma poultry trade with its engine room and stack in the rear so the heat wouldn't damage the perishable eggs in the bow.

Eventually the irrigation required for immense farms depleted the rivers, and the steamboat network shrank. Tugboats pulling barges took over river freight.

The Petaluma run was the last survivor of stern-wheeler ferryboat commerce in California. After he docked for the last time in Petaluma, Skipper Jack Urton, who had a flair for the historic moment, made a final entry in his log for August 24, 1950: "Arr. Petaluma 10:45 p.m. . . . After 35 year, 8 mo. and 10 days, we tie up for good. This ends 103 years of sternwheel river navigation on SF bay and tributaries.—John H. Urton, Master."

It was the railroad that really opened up the vast agricultural and timber regions to steady and lucrative trade. The narrow gauge through Marin and western Sonoma County carried vast amounts of timber to San Francisco markets. The Petaluma and Santa Rosa Electric Railway carried milk and apples from Sebastopol's Gold Ridge district to the Petaluma docks. Broad gauge lines in the Sonoma and Santa Rosa valleys gave Sonoma County farmers access to eastern markets, especially after refrigerated railroad cars were introduced to preserve perishable fruits, vegetables, and dairy products.

The first railroad enterprise was a modest one, however. In 1862, Minturn, the mogul of ferry traffic, improved his shipping system by laying three miles of track between Haystack Landing and Petaluma. The Petaluma and Haystack Railroad was the third railroad in the state.

Petalumans considered Minturn to be frugal to a fault, an opinion that was explosively confirmed when the train was about to leave Petaluma station on August 27, 1866. Minturn's regular engineer had quit, and substitute engineer Joe Levitt was in the cab firing up the Atlas locomotive. Minturn saved a few bucks by having Levitt act as fireman as well as engineer, but Levitt was apparently unaware it was his job to maintain the water level in the boiler. The boiler was bone dry, and when the steam gauge hit 120 pounds, the boiler blew. Pistons and chunks of locomotive flew in all directions. John McNear, one of Petaluma's leading citizens, had just bent over to tie his shoelace when a hunk of twisted metal whizzed over his head. The blast killed six men, including Levitt. Fortunately most passengers had left the platform and boarded the train, which shielded them from the cataclysm. Minturn never made good on his promise to replace the locomotive; for the rest of its 11-year history a team of horses pulled the P & H up and down the tracks.

As the 1860s drew to a close, Sonoma County had roughly 19,000 inhabitants, and most of them saw a railroad as their ticket to greater prosperity. Two routes had their partisans. Banker John Frisbie, General Vallejo's son-in-law, proposed a rail line from Vallejo to Cloverdale by way of Sonoma and Santa Rosa, a route that would freeze out Petaluma, the county's biggest town. Petalumans, naturally, favored a Petaluma-to-Cloverdale route. Sonoma County supervisors offered a subsidy of $5,000 per mile to the first company laying 10 miles of track.

One of the men to take up the challenge was Peter Donahue, an enterprising native of Glasgow, Scotland, who became a captain of industry after migrating in his late 20s to California during the gold rush. Starting as an ordinary machinist,

OPPOSITE, TOP: With the arrival of the railroad, production in the lumber industry increased dramatically. By 1886 a spur ran seven miles along Austin Creek to Cazadero, making accessible vast tracts of timberland owned by some of the railroad directors. Redwood was the primary freight. Courtesy, Don Silverek Photography

OPPOSITE, BOTTOM: George Guerne and Thomas Heald owned this large lumber mill in an area called Big Bottom (now known as Guerneville). In the 1870s the largest mill on the Sonoma coast was Duncans Mill, producing 25,000 feet of lumber per day. Courtesy, Don Silverek Photography

BELOW: Railroads came to Sonoma County in the 1870s, quickening the pulse of commerce and boosting trade with the Port of San Francisco. Courtesy, Don Silverek Photography

he created San Francisco's Union Iron Works, a prosperous factory that built mining equipment and locomotives. Then Donahue turned his boundless energy to railroading itself. Donahue purchased the San Francisco and North Pacific Railroad and built a line north from Petaluma toward Santa Rosa. Regular service on the line started in October 1870. On the last day of 1870 Donahue invited San Francisco bigwigs to an inaugural ride from Petaluma all the way to Santa Rosa.

Donahue continued to lay track north of Santa Rosa, but early in 1871 met his match. Frisbie had contributed $100,000 to the California Pacific Railroad to see a rail line built north via Sonoma Valley. Technically, the supervisors had committed themselves to a $5,000-a-mile subsidy to the first railroad laying a line all the way through the county. Soon the SF&NP and the Cal P were in a race toward Healdsburg along parallel tracks, Donahue's Irish workers digging madly on one side and Cal P's Chinese coolies swinging picks on the other. The

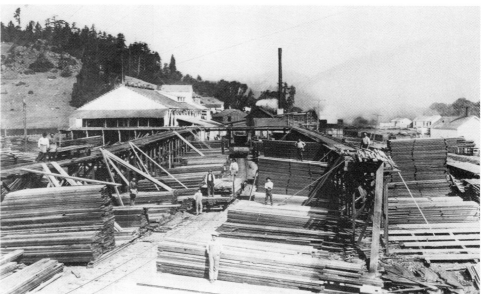

marathon came to an abrupt halt when Donahue sold out to Cal P for $750,000. Two years later he bought it back for a cool million. By then the rails ran all the way to Cloverdale.

The SF&NP line brought prosperity to Santa Rosa, Healdsburg, and the towns in central Sonoma County, but was too far east for the timbermen of the lower Russian River. George Guerne and Thomas Heald owned the largest mill in an area called Big Bottom, later called Stumptown (for obvious reasons), and finally known as Guerneville. Frank, Antoine, and Joseph Korbel had originally gone into the lumber business to build boxes for their San Francisco cigar business and wound up as timbermen. Together they went to Donahue, offering free wood for trestles if he would build a line to the heart of redwood country. Donahue built the Fulton and Guerneville Railroad in 1876, connecting to the SF&NP at Fulton.

A separate narrow-gauge line, linking communities in the western parts of Sonoma and Marin counties, began at the ferry terminal in Sausalito. Owners of the North Pacific Coast Railroad (later the North Shore and then Northwestern Pacific) felt the less expensive slim gauge could penetrate the region's dense forests and narrow canyons. By 1873 1,300 Chinese laborers were out with picks and shovels preparing the line while other workers built trestles over countless gulches. The Brown's Canyon trestle south of Howards was then the highest in the United States, and there were 68 other trestles between Point Reyes and Monte Rio. Freestone was the terminus for a couple of years while the workers graded the line up to the 575-foot summit at Howards (later Occidental), named after "Dutch Bill" Howard, one of the earliest settlers.

With the influx of railroad crews, Valley Ford and Freestone enjoyed a brief boomtown prosperity. Rancher Hollis Hinds built a 32-room hotel near the Freestone depot, and other hotels and rooming houses flourished. In Septebmer 1876 the railroad reached the Russian River at Monte Rio. Not everyone was glad the line was finished. Watchman T. Perry was on night duty in May 1877 when he spotted a trestle on fire near Freestone. Perry's nine-year-old boy roused a crowd who put the fire out before it consumed the bridge. The arsonist torched another trestle in August but this time section boss M. Shea caught the perpetrator red-handed. The culprit was Hinds, who hoped to save his hotel by drumming up some business from workmen who would stay in his hotel while they rebuilt the trestles.

Narrow-gauge locomotives

ABOVE: After tracks were laid in the 1870s, Bay Area residents could hop on ferries that connected to rail lines to Sonoma Valley or the Russian River. Here, tourists prepare to board the train at Monte Rio. Courtesy, Don Silverek Photography

LEFT: Resorts flourished along the tracks at Mirabel, Hilton, Rio Nido, Guerneville, Camp Meeker, Occidental, and Monte Rio, where this railroad trestle is located. Accommodations on the Russian River ranged from floored tents to multi-story hotels nestled among the redwoods. Sully's Resort in Monte Rio sent its autobus to the Monte Rio train station to collect guests. Courtesy, Don Silverek Photography

OPPOSITE: Bull teams were used to haul heavy timber in the early days of the lumber industry. This timber site near Occidental appears to have been stripped of its stand of timber. Courtesy, Sonoma County Museum

warmed up at the ferry building in Sausalito and chugged northwest toward Point Reyes, picking up clams and oysters from Marshall and Bivalve on the edge of Tomales Bay. At Tomales they picked up hay and milk before steaming through a tunnel and stopping at Valley Ford and Bodega for potatoes and hogs. North of Freestone the track entered timber country, cresting at Howards and then descending to the Russian River at Monte Rio. Steaming uphill, the locomotive made periodic stops to take on water; crew and passengers would hop off the train and toss some cordwood on board to replenish fuel for the engine.

Small mills had been turning out lumber for local use for years, but with the arrival of the railroad, production went into high gear. Mills like Streeten's and Tyrone flourished along the narrow-gauge line. In 1876 Alexander Duncan moved his mill several miles upstream to be near the railroad, settling at the present site of Duncans Mills.

By 1886 a spur ran 7.4 miles along Austin Creek to Cazadero, chiefly to take advantage of vast tracts of timber owned by some of the railroads' directors. Redwood, an ideal wood for buildings, was the primary freight. Tanbark oak, a wood that contained more tannin than any other tree, was another prized cargo. Chinese woodcutters and, later, newly arrived Italian immigrants would peel the tannin-bearing bark off in the spring when the sap was running, then cut the rest up for cordwood. Tanbark oak was an important Sonoma County product until the 1930s when a synthetic compound for tanning leather was developed in Germany.

The county-wide railroad network was a tremendous boon to farmers and businessmen. By the end of the century, Sonoma County was one of the most prosperous counties in the nation, the produce from its ranches and farms speeding to markets undreamed of in the mid-1800s.

Every summer adults and children practically lived in the fields, working all day to glean the thumb-sized hops from 15- to 20-foot vines. These families of hops pickers lived near the Russian River area in the late nineteenth century. Courtesy, Sonoma County Museum

Immigrants and Agriculture

With railroads to speed Sonoma County goods to market, several products came into their own. Sonoma County folks had harvested timber, apples, eggs, and dairy products for themselves, but suddenly these goods became big business with this quantum leap in transportation. And with the innovation of ice cars, Sonoma County produce could be rushed fresh to eastern markets. Agriculture flourished to such an extent that in the 1920 census Sonoma County was listed as the eighth most productive county in the United States. In 1937 it was still in 10th place.

Immigrants played key roles in the burgeoning industries. As the fabled land of opportunity, America lured adventurous souls from all the countries of the world, and Sonoma County drew more than its share. Italians, Swiss, Irish, British, Germans, Portuguese, and Chinese all played their part in nineteenth-century Sonoma County, just as other nationalities—Japanese, Mexicans, Ethiopians, Cambodians—would in the twentieth century.

No other immigrant group was so tied to the history of the railroads as the Chinese. Although some railroad tycoons like Peter Donahue refused to hire Orientals, a flood of Chinese came to California during the 1860s and 1870s. Hundreds of Chinese "coolies" worked on the narrow gauge through western Marin and Sonoma and stayed to work in timber, farming, or household jobs like cooking. By 1880, 125 Chinese had congregated to form a Santa Rosa Chinatown, and many more worked in rural areas.

While times were good the white population of California lived in uneasy coexistence with the Orientals. But the 1870s brought a widespread economic downturn that prompted whites to blame the Chinese for their economic woes. By 1886, disgruntled white workers clamored for the expulsion of California's quarter-million Chinese.

Prejudice found its way into the editorials of California's newspapers. "Go where you may in the state you find swarms of these people," editorialized the *Sonoma Democrat* in December 1885. "They are in every hotel, in nearly all private houses where servants are employed, in the laundries, in shops and stores, in the mines, on the farm—in fact everywhere. The population of the state is about one million, one-fourth of whom are Chinamen. Now it is evi-

dent that Chinese immigration must be stopped or the ruin of California is inevitable." Chinese were barred from becoming citizens and voters, and Governor George Stoneman stood firmly behind his white constituents, declaring that "the Chinese . . . are crowding the Caucasian race out of many avenues of employment."

Anti-Chinese associations and anti-coolie leagues sprang up all over California. Their common weapon was boycott. Santa Rosans met at the skating rink in January 1886, pledging to "rid themselves of the Chinese evil." The Healdsburg Anti-Coolie Club secured the signatures of 700 locals who vowed to withhold money from Chinese laborers and merchants.

Prejudice against Chinese in Sonoma County was further inflamed by a sensational murder near Cloverdale in January 1886. Jesse Wickersham and his wife were found shotgunned in their farmhouse, and their missing cook, Ah Tai, was blamed for the murder. Ah Tai vanished on a steamer leaving San Francisco, but he and, by association, his countrymen were tried in the papers. "The sentiment against the Chinese runs high in consequence of this act of heathen brutality, and the Chinese during yesterday kept in close quarters," reported the *Sonoma Democrat* on January 30, 1886. "Chinese cooks will find great difficulty in securing employment in this section of the country hereafter." In the wake of the murder, crowds turned out at mass meetings—2,000 in Petaluma and 1,000 in Cloverdale—to press for a universal boycott of Chinese businesses.

Prejudice had become a matter of law in 1882 when the federal government, bowing to pressure from California, ratified a new treaty with China that prohibited immigration of Chinese for 10 years. The ban was renewed in 1892 and 1902. Despite the widespread boycott of the 1880s, some early immigrants stayed on and found employment with sympathetic neighbors.

Like so many others, Italians came to California during the gold rush, and by 1851 there were about 600 Italians in San Francisco. Some rushed to Placer country, while others like Domenico Ghirardelli made a fortune in mercantile trades. In 1880 the cost of passage from Italy to New York dropped to $40; large numbers of Northern Italians migrated from Genoa and Turin and

ABOVE: Vineyard workers pick grapes for the Simi Brothers Winery in Healdsburg around 1900. Courtesy, Don Silverek Photography

OPPOSITE, TOP: Genoese banker Andrea Sbarbaro founded the Italian-Swiss Agricultural Colony at Asti in 1881. With chemist Pietro Rossi as his head winemaker, the colony began to prosper after a few lean years. Production was so abundant in 1897 that a 500,000-gallon capacity rock reservoir was built to store the wine. It is no wonder that workers received, in addition to wages, all the wine they could drink. Courtesy, Sonoma County Museum

OPPOSITE, BOTTOM: The grape harvest was a family affair throughout the 1800s and early 1900s. Here families harvest grapes in the Simi Vineyards at the turn of the century. Courtesy, Don Silverek Photography

the Lombard vineyard regions, bringing their expertise and passion for grape growing with them. Many bypassed the large eastern cities of the U.S. and headed straight for the slopes of California. The soil and climate of California are similar to that of Tuscany and other regions of Northern Italy. Farmers and vintners from the north of Italy found their pastoral life was readily transplanted to the slopes and valleys of Sonoma County. Between 1890 and 1920 a large influx of Italians settled in the Russian River Valley between Healdsburg and

Cloverdale to create winemaking dynasties.

The man who gave many Italian farmers their start in Sonoma County was Andrea Sbarbaro, a Genoese banker who envisioned a semi-utopian community for unemployed farmers from Italy and Switzerland. With chemist Pietro Rossi as his head winemaker, Sbarbaro founded the Italian-Swiss Agricultural Colony at Asti in 1881. Workers received wages plus all the wine they could drink. After a few lean years, the colony prospered. The 1897 vintage was so great that there was not enough cooperage in all of California to contain it. To store excess wine, Italian-Swiss constructed a solid rock reservoir 80 feet by 34 feet by 25 feet deep—the largest wine tank in the world, holding 500,000 gallons. When the tank was emptied in the spring of 1898, 200 workers held a dance inside it with an orchestra seated in the center. By 1910 Italian-Swiss had the largest capacity of any winery in the U.S.—8.5 million gallons.

Italian wine dynasties—the Sebastianis, Simis, Martinis, and Pratis—were the rule. But Italians did not have a monopoly on Sonoma County grape growing. German immigrant Jacob Gundlach was among the early wine growers in the Sonoma Valley. Gundlach left Germany in 1850 for California, but his plans did not include mining. He planted 400 acres of vineyards, constructed a stone winery on his Rhinefarm Estate near Sonoma, and in 1862 went into partnership with fellow Bavarian Charles Bundschu. Their wines gained a following, first in San Francisco, then on the East Coast, and by the turn of the century the Gundlach-Bundschu Wine Company warehouse in San Francisco covered an entire city block.

Pennsylvanian Isaac DeTurk came to Santa Rosa in 1862 and planted his first Yulupa Vineyard in 1862. By the 1880s his three cellars at Bennett Valley, Santa Rosa, and Cloverdale were producing 250,000 gallons of wine and 10,000 gallons of brandy a year. DeTurk's wines won four first places at the 1881 state fair. During the 1880s and 1890s he served as state viticultural commissioner for the Sonoma district.

DeTurk was also a pioneer in enlightened labor rela-

tions, criticizing other growers for their casual attitude toward field hands. "I think these proprietors are to blame for crowding the laborers into their barns like horses and cattle and allowing them to sleep out in their haystacks in the fields during harvest time," DeTurk wrote. "I have built a nice tenement house for my men and give them good food and a good table to eat at, and I find my men more willing to stop with me."

The three Korbel brothers, Francis, Anton, and Joseph, came to California from Czechoslovakia. Originally machinists and locksmiths, they turned to the cigar business and in the 1860s bought 6,000 acres of timber east of Guerneville to log wood for cigar boxes. Later they switched from timber to grapes, using the land they cleared along the Russian River. To satisfy the champagne taste of high-flying San Francisco society, the Korbels imported a champagne master from their homeland and became U.S. pioneers of the *méthode champenoise*—a style of making

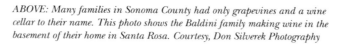

ABOVE: Many families in Sonoma County had only grapevines and a wine cellar to their name. This photo shows the Baldini family making wine in the basement of their home in Santa Rosa. Courtesy, Don Silverek Photography

TOP: Francis, Anton, and Joseph Korbel came to California from Czechoslovakia. Originally machinists and locksmiths, they turned to the cigar business and in the 1860s bought 6,000 acres of timberland east of Guerneville to log wood for cigar boxes. This photo depicts the Korbel sawmill, four miles north of Guerneville. The Korbels would later make their name in the wine industry. Courtesy, Don Silverek Photography

The Korbel Brothers diversified, and the prune industry was one of many activities at the site of their winery. Here prunes dry at the winery near Guerneville. Courtesy, Don Silverek Photography

ABOVE: *For decades, hops—an essential ingredient in beer—was a big crop in the area. Acres of rich floodland along the county's creeks were the prime areas for hop ranches. After the 1870s ranches sprang up along the Laguna de Santa Rosa and Santa Rosa Creek, as well as up and down the Russian River. Today Sonoma County's hop kilns are falling into ruin, although some have been transformed into picturesque settings for wineries. Courtesy, William Beedie Photo Collection*

OPPOSITE, TOP: *Prussian immigrant William Metzger started the Santa Rosa Steam Brewery in 1872, supplying saloons that sold beer for a nickel a glass. Frank and Joseph Grace bought Metzger out in 1897 to begin the Grace Brothers Brewing Company. Here, a group of Grace Brothers employees enjoy their product in front of the brewery. Courtesy, Don Silverek Photography*

OPPOSITE, BOTTOM: *Youngsters who picked hops for extra money were generally paid one cent per pound, and were able to pick perhaps 100 pounds of hops per day. Courtesy, Sonoma County Museum*

champagne directly in the bottle.

The wine industry continued to prosper. Agostin Haraszthy had shrewdly imported the pick of European vines in the 1860s. By the turn of the century Sonoma County was known through the country as a premier wine region. In 1875 the county produced almost 3.4 million gallons of wine, more than any county in California, a full 41 percent of the state's total wine production. (Napa County was fourth with a meager 873,000 gallons.) Wine grape tonnage for the county was 32,524 tons for 1890, and by 1910 it had more than doubled to 68,778. Before Prohibition, there were more than 200 wineries in the area and as many as 40,000 acres planted in vines.

The major setback to the industry was the phylloxera pest that also ravaged the vineyards of Europe. The pest, a louse that attacked the roots of the vines, did the greatest damage in the Sonoma Valley, showing up there around 1875. The infestation spread north and appeared in the

Russian River Valley by the 1890s. Growers tried flooding the vineyards or applying chemicals, but most eventually threw in the towel and dug up entire vineyards, replanting with resistant vines on which to graft their fine varieties. The grafting method worked; by the turn of the century Sonoma County vines were replanted and thriving.

Winemaking with its venerable old world traditions was perhaps the most prestigious Sonoma County enterprise, but other agricultural products came to prominence in the nineteenth century as well, among them hops, eggs, and apples.

Ranchers planted hops in the rich bottom land around the Russian River and the Laguna starting in the 1870s. Every August, men, women, and children moved out to the fields to glean hops from the 20-foot vines; the annual harvest took on the quality of a community festival, with families camping in the fields. Hop kilns, used for drying the crop, dotted the west county. (The best-preserved example is at Hop Kiln Winery, lovingly restored by owner Martin Griffin and listed on the National Register of Historic Places.) Hops put the bitter tang into beer, so breweries naturally sprang up not far from hop ranches. Prussian immigrant William Metzger started

With the hop ranches came beer, and basement bottling operations such as this one sprang up throughout the county. The Santa Rosa Steam Brewery, later known as Grace Brothers Brewing Company, began supplying beer to nearby saloons. Courtesy, Sonoma County Museum

the Santa Rosa Steam Brewery in 1872, supplying saloons that sold the suds for a nickel a glass. Frank and Joseph Grace bought Metzger out in 1897; Grace Brothers Brewing Company bottled beer under the Acme label, which became one of the state's favorite brands. Ranchers shipped hops in 200-pound bales to ports as far away as Australia.

Petaluma rose to prominence as the "Egg Capital of the World," largely through the efforts of two inventors

and an astute promoter. Canadian Lyman Byce came to Petaluma in 1878 and there perfected the modern incubator. The concept was centuries old, but Byce found a way to keep incubator temperatures steady. Byce's incubator went on display at the Sonoma-Marin Agricultural Society Fair in 1879, and it was a big hit at the 1883 state fair. The aisles of the exhibit pavilion were packed with curious onlookers who crowded around the incubator to watch chicks emerging from their shells. Ladies, caught between the warm incubators and the pressing crowds, fainted from the heat, and watchmen reported many visitors left the pavilion with cheeping sounds coming from their pockets.

Christopher Nisson, a native of Schleswig-Holstein on the German-Danish border, came to Petaluma in 1864 and raised brown leghorns in Two Rock. Using Byce's new incubator, he hatched chicks for his neighbors; by the 1880s Nisson had 2,000 laying hens and was the region's first commercial egg rancher. Nisson developed a better brooder using better ventilation, and he developed a balanced feed for poultry. His articles on chicken raising drew experts from all over Europe. In 1898 Nisson moved his equipment to the town of Petaluma and founded the Pioneer Hatchery, America's first commercial hatchery. With improved incubators and brooders, Petaluma became a leading poultry center as rival hatcheries were established.

It was not until 1918, however, that Petaluma consciously billed itself as the world's egg basket. At the close of World War I, Petaluma's Chamber of Commerce hired H.W. Kerrigan to survey the town's industrial potential. To their surprise, Kerrigan advised the town fathers to put all their eggs in one basket and promote the poultry business.

Petaluma, calculated Kerrigan, had more hatcheries and poultry breeding farms than anywhere else in the world. Under his direction the chamber spent $50,000 to publicize Petaluma as the "Egg Capital of the World." They invited national newsreel companies to film chicken and egg scenes and the town's Egg Day parades. Petaluma eggs were shipped worldwide.

Hundreds of ranchers came down with chicken fever and moved to the area to start their own ranches with a few hundred chickens each. Among them was a group of Jewish socialists who came to Petaluma to establish a rural community, seeing agricultural life as a haven for refugees from the sweatshops of eastern cities. The first Jewish families came to Petaluma before 1915; the next year they helped organize a Poultry Producers cooperative that also served as a savings bank. By 1925 there were 100 Jewish

ABOVE: In 1918 Petaluma consciously started billing itself as the world's egg basket. At the close of World War I, the Petaluma Chamber of Commerce hired H.W. Kerrigan to survey the town's industrial potential and suggest a new direction. Kerrigan discovered that Petaluma had more hatcheries and poultry breeding farms than anywhere else in the world. Courtesy, Don Silverek Photography

LEFT: Catalog shopping was the primary method of obtaining "Things you need" in the late 1800s and early 1900s. This ad from Catalogue No. 47 marketed the improved incubators that were responsible for establishing Petaluma as a leading poultry center. By 1904 the Petaluma Hatchery had a capacity for hatching 500,000 eggs at once. Courtesy, Sonoma County Museum

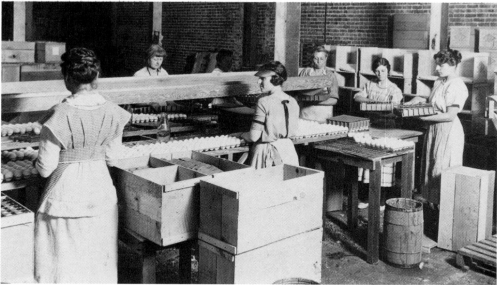

ABOVE: *Women work at an egg packing plant in Petaluma in the early 1900s. Courtesy, Don Silverek Photography*

TOP: *Under the direction of H.W. Kerrigan, the Petaluma Chamber of Commerce spent $50,000 to publicize Petaluma as the "Egg Capital of World." National newsreel companies filmed hatcheries and the town's Egg Day parades. This horse-drawn chicken was photographed in about 1920. Courtesy, Don Silverek Photography*

ABOVE: Although the Russians at Fort Ross introduced the Gravenstein apple to the region, it was orchardist Nathaniel Griffith who proved that the Gravenstein was a viable commercial crop, establishing the nearby Gold Ridge region as their rightful home. The industry soon grew, providing jobs in packing houses like the Apple Co-op Packing House in Forestville. Courtesy, Don Silverek Photography

ABOVE: To promote their star crop, Sebastopol ranchers organized the first Gravenstein Apple Show in 1910. Sebastopol Mayor James P. Kelly kicked off the speeches, introducing the guest of honor, California Governor James Gillet. Music concessions and "riding devices" entertained the crowd until midnight. A confetti fight concluded the event on the final evening. Courtesy, Don Silverek Photography

RIGHT: Luther Burbank was well known for his development of many new varieties of plants and flowers. After 1875 he conducted his work in Sonoma County; he is pictured here in his garden at his Santa Rosa home. Courtesy, Don Silverek Photography

FACING PAGE: Sebastopol was, and still is, the world capital of the Gravenstein apple. Gravensteins were first introduced to the region by the Russians at Fort Ross. Orchardist Nathaniel Griffith planted Gravensteins near Sebastopol in the 1880s and was the first to introduce them as a viable commercial crop. To promote their star crop, Sebastopol ranchers organized the first Gravenstein Apple Show in 1910. Models built of apples were the highlight of the 1911 show, such as this all-apple model of the steam-powered paddlewheeler, the Gold. Courtesy, Sonoma County Museum

families and a Jewish community center.

In 1910 Petaluma shipped 7 million dozen eggs to San Francisco. Production hit a peak in 1929 and then slumped, but in 1940 Petaluma shipped out 30 million dozen eggs, not far behind the record high of the 1920s. Petaluma also had the distinction of having a drug store devoted entirely to chickens. The Chicken Pharmacy, founded in 1929 by James Keyes, at one time dispensed 50,000 pullet pills a day. The store was featured in a 1939 issue of the *National Geographic*.

If Petaluma was the world's egg capital, Sebastopol was the world capital of the apple, or at least the Gravenstein apple. Fort Ross's Russians introduced "Gravs" to

Sonoma County, but it was orchardist Nathaniel Griffith in the 1880s who first planted Gravensteins in the Gold Ridge section. He proved the apple was practical as a commercial crop, earning himself the nickname "Grandfather of the Gravenstein."

By 1910, the year of the first Gravenstein Apple Show, Sebastopol had a population of 2,000 and the surrounding Gold Ridge district, with its rich, sandy soil, was devoted to apple orchards. Gravensteins ship well and ripen early. Growers picked in July and shipped the fruit to eastern markets. "We have no authentic proof to give, that the Garden of Eden was located in the Gold Ridge Region," wrote Anna Morrison Reed, editor of Petaluma's

Northern Crown magazine, "but it looks reasonable that it might have been since it is now a Paradise of orchards and homes."

The Gravenstein Apple Fair was a prime force in promoting the tart apples. In 1910, the year of the first apple fair, there were 5,700 acres planted in apples. By 1920 the county boasted 27,000 acres in apples. In the midst of the Depression Sonoma County was still shipping 50,000 tons of dried apples and 1.5 million boxes of fresh apples annually.

Growers made sure the second annual Gravenstein fair, held in 1911, was even more of an extravaganza than the first one. The electric railway offered special rates to Sebastopol, where concert bands and a "Great Midway" entertained the crowds. Japanese orchardists constructed a replica of the "Mikado's Palace" built entirely of apples. Famed horticulturist Luther Burbank kicked off the fair by pressing an electric button that lit up the pavilion and set the industrial exhibits in motion. "The Gravenstein apple has, above all others, proved to be the money winner in Sonoma County," commented Burbank, who had an experimental farm on the outskirts of Sebastopol. "It cannot be raised successfully in the hot valleys of Southern California. Sonoma County seems to be its home."

Burbank, the wizard of plant breeding, was the image of the practical American genius. Like Thomas Edison, who visited Burbank's garden in 1915, Burbank had remarkable persistence and an uncanny talent for perceiving the results of his experiments. A master of the empirical rather than the theoretical, Burbank contributed to the world of horticulture by inventing more than 800 new varieties of plants.

Born in Massachusetts in 1849, Burbank grew up on a farm. After high school he was largely self-taught, influenced in particular by Charles Darwin's *The Variation of Animals and Plants Under Domestication*. At age 21 he bought a farm in Massachusetts and embarked on a

55-year career of experimentation, finding his first fame with the "Burbank potato." In 1875 Burbank traded the rights to his potato for a ticket to Sonoma County, where he spent the remainder of his life devising new strains of plants on his farms in Santa Rosa and Sebastopol. Burbank achieved notoriety for sensational discoveries like the white blackberry and spineless cactus, which was a big hit at the 1908 Cloverdale Citrus Fair. But Burbank's less publicized work was more significant: he developed more than 100 new varieties of prunes and plums, 50 types of lilies, and 10 varieties of commercial berries.

Burbank's celebrated wizardry lay in keen observation of the differences between plants he was breeding. He turned the diversity of nature to his advantage, encouraging some traits and weeding out others, to create entirely new strains of plants. His guest book was a catalog of the world's celebrities, and his restored house and garden in Santa Rosa across from Juilliard Park are still popular attractions. Never was so much practical genius assembled in one place as on October 11, 1915, when Thomas Edison, Harvey Firestone, and Henry Ford, visiting the West Coast for the Panama-Pacific International Exposition, made a detour to walk the garden paths with Burbank.

Author Jack London spoke for his fellow visitors when he wrote in Burbank's guest book, "I'd rather do what you're doing than be Roosevelt, Rockefeller, King Edward or the Kaiser rolled into one."

London, another Sonoma County celebrity in his own time, dabbled in some farming of his own near Glen Ellen in the Valley of the Moon, where he settled in 1910 on a spread he named the Beauty Ranch. There he delved into experimental farming with the same intensity he brought to all his endeavors, designing and building a concrete "piggery" for raising hogs. "I go into farming because my philosophy and research have taught me to recognize the fact that a return to the soil is the basis of economics," he wrote. "Do you realize that I devote two hours a day to writing and ten to farming?"

Of all Sonoma County's authors past and present, none is more widely read than London, whose own life was an adventure yarn as colorful as his books. Born in 1876, he spent his teens sailing San Francisco Bay as an oyster pirate. Handsome, confident, and charismatic, he hurled himself into life's experiences. He traveled the country on freight trains as a hobo; signed on as an able-bodied seaman for Japan and the Bering Sea; and joined the Alaska gold rush of 1897 as a prospector in the Klondike.

OPPOSITE: Well-known American author Jack London chose to settle in Sonoma County in his later years. London was born in San Francisco and at the age of 17 shipped as a seaman to Japan and the Bering Sea. He later became a newspaper correspondent during the Russo-Japanese war and a war correspondent in Mexico. His stories had begun to appear in magazines when The Son of the Wolf *was published in 1900. Courtesy, Don Silverek Photography*

BELOW: While Jack London was well known for his many books and writings, many did not know that he had an interest in livestock. He raised pigs on his ranch in the Valley of the Moon. Pictured here is the "Piggery," the stone pig barn designed by London. Courtesy, Don Silverek Photography

ABOVE: Thomas Lake Harris, the first of the Utopians in Sonoma County, established his 1,400-acre Fountaingrove colony just north of Santa Rosa. The community was a prosperous one, with a book press and winery. Harris began his "Brotherhood of the New Life" in New York State and moved to his "new Eden of the West" in 1875. As the commune's last survior, Japanese nobleman Kanay Nagasawa inherited the estate, but anti-alien laws prevented Nagasawa from leaving Fountaingrove to his heirs. Baron Nagasawa appears here with relatives at Fountaingrove Ranch. Courtesy, Sonoma County Museum

London quit school at 14, but he haunted the Oakland Public Library and was largely self-taught. After his Alaskan adventures he found a market for his adventure novel *Son of the Wolf* (1900), followed by an outpouring of 50 books—novels, memoirs, ballads, and stories. Having experienced a childhood of intense poverty, London became a life-long crusader against exploitation, an ardent socialist who typically signed his letters, "Yours for the revolution." Like many celebrities, he essentially created himself, and the self he created was the Proletarian Hero who rose from nothing through hard work.

Although he was at one time the highest paid author in the country, London's schemes were always more grandiose than his royalties, and he wrote constantly to stay ahead of his debts. At the Beauty Ranch London and his wife, Charmian, designed Wolf House, a three-story mansion of wood and stone, but days before its completion someone torched the house. London never fully recovered from the setback. His health declined, aggravated by overindulgence in food and drink, until he died in 1916. The ruins of Wolf House remain in Jack London State Park, not far from the House of Happy Walls, built by Charmian as a tribute to Jack.

Sonoma County, with its fertile valleys and gentle climate, had all the prerequisites of "heaven on earth," attracting many utopians in the nineteenth century who dreamed of establishing ideal communities. In the late 1800s, of nine established communes in California, four were in Sonoma County.

The first of the religious and social reformers to put down roots in the county was Thomas Lake Harris, who

built his 1,400-acre Fountaingrove colony just north of Santa Rosa. Preaching a combination of Christianity and spiritualism, Harris began the Brotherhood of the New Life in New York State, then moved to his "new Eden of the West" in 1875. The community was a prosperous one, with a book press and winery. The wine was not only a financial success, but Harris believed the Fountaingrove vintage, made in the spirit of devotion, was infused with the "substance of Divine and celestial energy." Harris encouraged wealthy followers to pour assets into the communal coffers. These financial arrangements, combined with Harris' arcane views about sex and mysticism, eventually proved to be his undoing. Two visitors claimed Harris made sexual advances to them and made slaves of his fol-

ABOVE: Schools were usually named for the district in which they were located. These children are taking time out for exercise and relaxation in front of the Freestone District School. Note some of the students are barefoot. Courtesy, the Ray Van Skyke Collection

OPPOSITE, TOP: Parades were a major source of entertainment at the turn of the century. There was no end to the imagination invested in parade floats, such as this one seen in front of the courthouse and the Bank of Italy in Santa Rosa. Courtesy, Don Silverek Photography

ABOVE: The All American Sport was enjoyed by young people very early in the settlement of the county. These young men are representatives of Petaluma's 1905 high school baseball team. Courtesy, Sonoma County Museum

OPPOSITE: Athletics were an important part of school life. The Santa Rosa High School track team posed in their uniforms in 1901. Courtesy, Sonoma County Museum

lowers. They touched off a campaign of innuendo in the press that drove Harris from Fountaingrove in 1892.

Kanay Nagasawa, a Japanese nobleman, was the eventual heir to the Fountaingrove legacy. As a boy he and 14 other sons of nobles were smuggled out of Japan to learn the ways of the West, despite the ban on travel in or out of Japan. The others all returned to become leaders of westernized Japan, but Nagasawa joined Harris and remained at Fountaingrove all his life. As the commune's last surviving member, he inherited the estate and reigned as the Baron of Fountaingrove until his death in 1934. It was Nagasawa who built the "Round Barn," now one of Santa Rosa's landmarks. An accomplished viticulturalist, he traded advice with Luther Burbank and encouraged rapport between his adopted country and Japan, especially his home province of Kagoshima. Today Sonoma County's

Friends of Kagoshima maintain a cordial exchange with their counterparts in Japan.

French Utopians interested in social rather than religious reform began the Icaria Speranza commune south of Cloverdale in 1881. The 55 members, all French speakers, worked together in fields and vineyards, hoping to abolish inequality by holding goods in common. Within a few years debts from previous Icarian farms swamped the Sonoma County commune. Armand Dehay, writing to fel-

low Icarian Alexis Marchand, lamented, "My heart is broken to see that our Commune collapsed like a house built on sand."

The Altrurians launched another short-lived communal experiment in 1894. Enthused by the novel *A Traveler from Altruria* by William Dean Howell, which fused Christian morality with socialism, the members chipped in $50 apiece to found an ethical community on a 185-acre parcel on Mark West Creek. Altruria boasted a weaving operation and print shop; it had grandiose plans for a quarry and a hotel. Idealism and prosperity aren't necessarily mutually exclusive, but they were in Altruria's case. Perpetually in the red, the Altrurians amicably went their separate ways in 1895.

The fourth commune was not a deliberate colony but a group of devotees who clustered around the magnetic Madame Emily Preston at her ranch north of Cloverdale. A renowned herbalist, Madame Preston prescribed salves, potions, and doses of her own elderberry wine. Easterners came to see her at the Preston Ranch or at a San Francisco apartment she kept for consultations. Patients believed she could diagnose them by looking into their eyes, and 100 followers became so attached to her that they stayed permanently. She allowed them to build on her land for free and pick fruit from her orchards. Madame Preston's religious code consisted of straightforward pronouncements like, "Condemn no church. Have no discord. Strive for unity." A writer for the *San Francisco Chronicle* in 1887 commented on her influence: "Her hallucination, if it be a hallucination, has a tendency only to elevate." When she died in 1909, aged 90, the *Cloverdale Reveille* called her "a much beloved woman."

A Rose Carnival and parade restored Santa Rosans' post-earthquake spirits in the spring of 1907. The traditional Rose Carnival, heralding the awakening of the sleeping earth from the long dormant winter, has been a tradition since the 1800s and features roses and spring blossoms in its events and parade. Children were the primary participants in the parade. These young girls displaying new dresses and glowing smiles are Alice Cullin, Claire Coltrin, Margaret Forsythe, and Zelma Carithers. Courtesy, Sonoma County Library

Quake to 1940

It was a quiet Wednesday morning, 5:13 a.m., in Santa Rosa. Travelers at the Occidental Hotel and the Saint Rose were still asleep, and out on the street paper boys were making their rounds. Forty-eight seconds later, on the morning of April 18, 1906, virtually every business in downtown Santa Rosa was in ruins and most of the homes were damaged.

Although the quake is known as the Great San Francisco Earthquake, no city suffered as much damage proportionally as Santa Rosa. The next day a joint edition of three San Francisco newspapers—the *Call, Chronicle,* and *Examiner*—carried a story announcing, "Santa Rosa Is a Total Wreck." While some Sonoma County towns stand on stable bedrock, Santa Rosa was built on loose deposits of alluvium that shook like jello. The entire downtown section collapsed in a pile of loose bricks. The 2,000-seat Athenaeum theatre was a shambles, and the four-story courthouse with its impressive dome collapsed like a fallen wedding cake. Inside the Presbyterian Church on Humboldt, the massive chandelier swayed and fell, crushing empty seats that had been full of worshippers three mornings before on Easter Sunday. The town's water system was in ruins, dooming the Santa Rosa Fire Department's efforts to combat the resulting blazes.

Over 100 people died in Santa Rosa, many in the collapse of the town's three large hotels, the Occidental, the Saint Rose, and the Grand. "They fell as if constructed of playing cards, and in the heaps were buried the hundreds of lodgers," reported the San Francisco papers. The Sonoma County Library has a microfilm copy of a *Press Democrat* delivered minutes before the cataclysm; someone scrawled across the top of the front page, "The boy who handled this paper was killed in the quake."

Damage was widespread. The new Masonic Hall in Windsor was destroyed. The towns of Tomales and Bloomfield were in ruins. Three workers at the Great Eastern quicksilver mine near Guerneville were crushed by falling rocks, and in Occidental brick chimneys tumbled from every roof in town. La Bonita Hotel in Duncans Mills crumpled to the ground, and the Fort Ross chapel, built directly over the San Andreas Fault, collapsed. The entire Point Reyes peninsula jumped 17 feet northward, knocking the Point Reyes lighthouse off its mount and upsetting the delicate mechanism of the revolving Fresnel lens. Out

at sea the skipper of the *Alliance,* steaming past Eureka, felt the sudden jolt and thought his ship had run aground.

In San Francisco, most damage was done by fires that swept the city after the earthquake. Firefighting was hampered by ruptured water mains. Sonoma County winemakers learned their vast warehouses in the city were destroyed. Winemaker Charles Bundschu, writing to a friend days after the quake, lamented, "Our building fell at 5 o'clock on the first day. When we got the news, my tears fell incessantly . . . It meant the labor and struggle of two generations, and now—and now?" Italian-Swiss Colony was luckier. The quake ruined 10 million gallons of wine but the warehouse near Telegraph Hill was saved from fire because of a natural spring underneath. For several days the "lake" at the Italian-Swiss warehouse was one of the chief sources of fresh water in the city.

Towns with less damage sent help to Santa Rosa. Petaluma's Elks Lodge and its chamber of commerce each sent a carload of provisions. Sebastopol sent a fire engine. On Sunday the Fitch family rode in with a wagonload of provisions from Calistoga's Red Cross Society. The Northwestern Pacific Railroad offered its wrecking crew with a derrick and steam shovel to clear away the debris of downtown.

Santa Rosans were quick to dust themselves off and carry on with their lives. The Sunday after the quake, Presbyterians carried their chairs and reed organ to a vacant lot behind the church and held outdoor services. The following day students returned to the Santa Rosa Business College, and workers were erecting a temporary city hall on the Native Sons' lot on Mendocino Avenue. Within a week the *Press Democrat* leased a lot on Mendocino formerly occupied by a Chinese washhouse and started on a new building. Paul Hahman's ledger, with entries written in his elegant script, shows business at his drug store was interrupted for only two days. Hahman's Apothecary had the first plate glass window in Santa Rosa's new downtown. Local newspapers, once started printing makeshift editions, were full of news about mercantile ventures rising from the ashes. Much of the stock of businesses like Mailer's Hardware and Bacigalupi's Grocery had been saved. Within a week most Fourth Street merchants set up shop at home or in temporary quarters. Train cars full of brick

and lumber arrived to construct the new improved Santa Rosa.

City fathers, mustering as much optimism as anyone could under the circumstances, looked on the disaster as a kind of unplanned urban renewal. "For a long time it has been generally recognized that the majority of Santa Rosa's business streets were too narrow, and now that the opportunity for widening them has arrived it must be embraced," reasoned an April 30 editorial in the jointly issued *Santa Rosa Democrat-Republican.* "It will only be a few years until electric cars are occupying all our principal streets . . ."

The city council, convening two days after the disaster, announced its intentions to "Build a bigger and better Santa Rosa." A *Press Democrat* editorial on April 23 commented on the need for a new courthouse, adding, "While we are about it, we might as well build it right. A modern up-to-date structure is the only thing that will fill the bill." The quake had destroyed nineteenth-century Santa Rosa; a twentieth-century town rose from the rubble.

Even before the quake, Sonoma County residents had felt the tremors of a different kind of upheaval: the social reform movement that discouraged drinking. Defenders of saloons saw them as social clubs for the working man; reformers condemned them as part of a cycle of crime and poverty. An unlikely opponent of dry laws was Anna Morrison Reed, editor of Petaluma's *Northern Crown* magazine. A supporter of social reform and a founding member of the Pacific Coast Women's Press Association, Reed nevertheless toured the country lecturing against prohibition. "The whole world is, at this time undergoing an agitation, and attempted reform, at the hands of 'professed moralists,'" Reed wrote in her magazine in 1916. "Any attempted national prohibition . . . would result in a practical failure, because all experience demonstrates that the mass of the people will not tolerate such regulation." Reed also brought up an argument that carried plenty of weight in Sonoma County. Alcohol was big business. Eight hundred wineries in California were in jeopardy, as were the state's 60 breweries that used 80,000 pounds of barley and over a million pounds of hops a year. Sonoma County, heavily depen-

dent on grapes and hops, faced economic disaster.

The call to ban alcohol gained momentum after 1900; by 1917 two-thirds of the states had adopted individual prohibition laws. During World War I Congress banned the sale of intoxicants to conserve grain supplies and then drafted an Eighteenth Amendment to the U.S. Constitution barring sale and manufacture of alcoholic beverages. The states quickly ratified it and Congress passed the Volstead Act to enforce it. Comic Will Rogers summed up the contradictions of the years to follow: "If you think this country ain't dry, just watch 'em vote. If you think this country ain't wet, just watch 'em drink. You see when they vote it's counted, but when they drink it ain't."

Prohibition began in January 1920. A January 16 *Press Democrat* headline announced that "John Barleycorn Is Breathing His Last Here Today." On the first Sunday of the dry era, parishioners at St. Rose's Catholic Church in Santa Rosa were startled by the week's selection from holy scripture. It was the passage from the Gospel of John telling how Jesus turned water into wine for the wedding guests at Cana.

Locally, winemakers wondered what to do with three million gallons of wine, stored in Sonoma County vats, which could not legally be sold or moved. Librarians puz-zled over whether to whisk books on winemaking off the shelves. One thing soon became apparent: people would exercise their imaginations to get around the new law.

The Volstead Act permitted citizens to make 200 gallons for home use, so there was still a market for grapes. In fact, by 1930 cultivation of grapes actually rose to 30,000 acres. But times were hard for wineries; between 1920 and 1933, when the act was repealed, Sonoma County lost two-thirds of its more than 200 wineries. The Bundschu family closed its winery and harvested grapes for others. Sebastiani's in Sonoma survived by concentrating on medicinal and sacramental wines, which were legal, and by shipping

OPPOSITE, TOP: The dome of the Sonoma County courthouse collapsed in the great earthquake of 1906. Courtesy, Don Silverek Photography

OPPOSITE, BOTTOM: The earthquake of 1906 dealt a devastating blow to what had seemed to be sound structures, including the Santa Rosa Free Public Library, which was constructed of stone. Courtesy, Sonoma County Museum

BELOW: San Francisco's newspapers estimated the 1906 earthquake death toll in Santa Rosa would be in the thousands. Fortunately, this was not true. The actual count of lives lost in Santa Rosa was 103—many of them were lodgers in Santa Rosa's three largest hotels. Pictured is the coroner's wagon waiting for victims to be pulled from the ruins of the Occidental Hotel in Santa Rosa. Courtesy, Sonoma County Museum

grapes back east to home winemakers. Italian-Swiss Colony made grape drinks and printed a pamphlet, "Is Entertaining a Lost Art?," to promote them. The pamphlet will "undoubtedly fill a need and make one realize that after all things are not 'as dark as they seem,'" the winemakers wistfully wrote. The booklet (preserved in the California Historical Society Library) included recipes for wine jelly and offered dining advice such as serving "Riesling type" beverages with oysters.

Saloons closed their doors and reopened as restaurants and stores. Some breweries, like Brandt's in Healdsburg, folded during Prohibition. Others, like Santa Rosa's

Grace Brothers, weathered the dry era as ice houses and bottling plants. Ranchers continued to grow hops; the crop's banner year was 1931 with 21,000 acres of hops planted in Sonoma County. Sonoma County beer drinkers weren't left high and dry. "During Prohibition everybody had their own little hop patches and made beer," remembered George Proctor, whose family owned seven hop ranches and at one time controlled half the hops in the state. "People drank more during Prohibition than they do now."

The county had its share of bootleggers and clandestine hooch. One local minister lamented that Sonoma

County was "wet, very wet." He urged his flock to dry out and wring the alcohol out of the rest of the community, too, by informing if need be. A tip led lawmen to one of their biggest busts in April 1931, when Sheriff Mike Flohr, District Attorney Emmett Donohue, and a small posse burst in on a distilling operation near the Laguna. Three surprised moonshiners left the boilers going full tilt and made a getaway in a rowboat. When the lawmen fired a few shots in the air, the trio leapt from the boat and scrambled away through the Laguna's knee-high muddy water. The posse nabbed two bootleggers but the third escaped, leaving behind his muddy trousers. The sheriff confiscated a thousand gallons of alcohol, 30,000 gallons of ferment-

By the start of the 1930s, the national mood had shifted. President Herbert Hoover was staunchly behind Prohibition, but his 1932 challenger, Franklin Roosevelt, was just as strongly against it. FDR's election was closely followed by repeal of Prohibition. "We voted for Roosevelt in 1932 to get beer back and we got it," remembered "Babe" Wood, a third-generation hop rancher whose grandfather started one of the county's first ranches in the 1870s. Sonoma County hop ranchers, grape growers, and vintners toasted their renewed good fortune and got to work. Trucks from Grace Brothers Brewery rolled again, each with a banner proclaiming "Happy Days Are Here Again."

ing mash, 100 sacks of sugar, and the still.

Much of the illegal liquor was smuggled into the country. On the north coast, ships from Vancouver anchored offshore just outside the international limit. When darkness fell a small boat would speed a shipment onto the beaches or even right through the Golden Gate. Along the isolated Sonoma coast north of Jenner, the doghole ports once used for loading timber proved handy for unloading booze. When the coast highway from Jenner to Gualala was completed in the late 1920s, rumrunners could make quick trips to the city from smugglers' coves at Salt Point and present-day Sea Ranch.

ABOVE:: The Pacific Telephone and Telegraph staff poses in front of their building in 1922, bringing communications to Sonoma County. Courtesy, Sonoma County Museum

OPPOSITE: Neighborhood movie theaters were the main source of entertainment before the advent of television. In addition to feature films, they offered live shows, newsreels, and cartoons. Santa Rosa had the Cline, the California, and the Roxy on B Street, the Strand on Davis Street, and the Elite and the Rose on Fourth Street. Admission in the 1940s was only 20 cents and popcorn was only five cents. Cash night at the California theater in Santa Rosa attracted throngs of people, as pictured in this photo. Courtesy, Sonoma County Library

"Babe" Wood constructed the building at the corner of Mendocino and Seventh in 1935 to house his REO truck franchise and later acquired DeSoto and Plymouth franchises. He eventually dropped Plymouth and acquired Pontiac and Cadillac, remaining in the same building from 1935 to 1976, when the dealership was moved to 2925 Corby Avenue, where it is still operating today. "Babe" Wood is still involved in the family business, which is presently operated by his son, Samuel. Courtesy, Sonoma County Library

But for hop growers the happy days were not to last. Beer was as popular as ever, but people preferred a lighter tasting brew. Hops, which gives beer its strong, bitter taste, was less in demand. Local ranchers also found it hard to compete with large-scale hop operations that sprang up in the Central Valley after World War II. The final blow to Sonoma County hop ranching was downy mildew. Coastal fog kept the hop vines too moist, and ranchers began to lose half their crops to the damp. By the 1960s hops, once a major Sonoma County crop, weren't profitable anymore. Grace Brothers Brewery shut down in the 1960s. Ranchers rolled with the times, converting their ranches to prune orchards and vineyards.

After Prohibition's repeal, county grape growers raised bulk wine grapes for bottlers outside the county. Small and medium-sized wineries popped up in Dry Creek, Alexander Valley, and along the Russian River. But the wine industry had suffered a setback. In Sonoma County, the grape harvest had peaked at 68,778 tons in 1910. In 1930 it had fallen to 33,934 tons a year, and 1940 saw only 29,425 tons of grapes produced. The wine industry would not fully recover until Americans turned wholeheartedly to wine drinking after the 1960s.

By the 1930s Americans had more to worry about than alcohol. The stock market crash of 1929 sent the world economy into a decade-long tailspin. Farmers from the drought-ravaged Dust Bowl migrated to California's valleys in hopes of work. FDR's New Deal, an alphabet soup of federal agencies designed to keep people working, funded many Sonoma County projects. A WPA (Works Progress Administration) grant paid Richard Brooks and Dorothy Wolf to conduct research on Sonoma County itself. After digging through archives and interviewing old timers, they wrote *Sonoma County: History and Description,* and *Foreign Born in Sonoma County,* a study of immigrants, both published by the WPA in 1936. The Public Works Administration kicked in half the money to put up a new firehouse in Santa Rosa. The WPA did $20,000 worth of work to prevent flooding on the Russian River and allocated $8,000 to spruce up the Sonoma County Fairgrounds with shrubbery and paint. Another New Deal brainchild was the CCC (Civilian Conservation Corps), an army of young men who earned $30 a month for forestry work and building projects ($25 went back home to their families). CCC boys lived in rural barracks resembling summer camps. They built bridges and walls as well as the amphitheater in Armstrong Woods. Materials were scarce so the camps often produced their own. "We had a pipe factory and made our own pipe, and did a lot of drainage work, too," remembers Marty Coorpender, a Santa Rosan who lived at Camp Sebastopol.

A major beneficiary of federal largesse was Santa Rosa Junior College, founded in 1918. The initial student body was 19, with eight faculty. At the time Santa Rosa had a population of 13,000 and boasted a high school, a junior high, and four grammar schools. For several years the junior college shared facilities with Santa Rosa High School. The college got its own Mendocino Avenue campus in 1931. The 40-acre site was originally earmarked as a park and was a favorite spot of Luther Burbank. Co-owners of the property, the city of Santa Rosa and the Santa Rosa Chamber of Commerce, agreed to locate SRJC there with a proviso for a 350-foot setback along Mendocino Avenue to preserve the park-like setting of oaks and flowers.

Santa Rosa Junior College was originally intended as an extension of UC Berkeley and had the same requirements, although in the 1930s its program expanded to encompass vocational training. Two early champions of the new school were Genevieve Mott and Clarence "Red" Tauzer. Mott was an English instructor in 1918, dean of women during the 1920s, and one of those most responsi-

ble for holding the school together in its early years. Tauzer, a graduate of Stanford Law School, coached football and basketball in the school's early years and served as perennial liaison between the college and the community. He was one of the school's biggest boosters until his death in 1948. Although the Depression meant hard times in general, it was the time of greatest expansion for the junior college. In 1938 Public Works Administration funds built three of the school's red brick, ivy-covered buildings —Analy Hall, Burbank Auditorium, and Bussman Hall— with a quarter-million-dollar bond.

Not all federal projects were so eagerly welcomed. When the Farm Security Administration planned to construct a model migrant workers' camp in Windsor in 1938,

These young men and women were students at the Santa Rosa Business College in the 1920s. Courtesy, Sonoma County Museum

county supervisors joined local farmers in loud objections. Housing for the laborers would be controlled not by the county but by the government, and that didn't sit well with local farmers and businessmen. Despite the objections, the government built Camp Windsor for 250 people, mostly Dust Bowl families in search of seasonal work.

The legacy of bad feeling between farm owners and farm workers stemmed partly from an ugly incident in 1935 when two union organizers were literally tarred and feathered. Farmers blamed labor organizers for fomenting a strike during the fruit and hop harvest, and early in August 1935 anti-labor toughs broke up a strike meeting at Santa Rosa's Germania Hall,

The female jurors in this June 1920 photo were the first women to sit on a jury in Sonoma County. Courtesy, Sonoma County Library

throwing the leaders out into the street. Two weeks later, labor leaders got wind that another meeting would be broken up, so they stayed home. As a result, frustrated anti-unionists broke up into small packs and rode to several spots around the county to kidnap the unionists, bringing them to a Santa Rosa warehouse. There they tarred and feathered Jack Green and Sol Nitzberg and threatened the rest. Green and Nitzberg told their woes to the Sonoma County Grand Jury, but the county district attorney declined to prosecute, citing lack of evidence. Then California Attorney General U.S. Webb, overriding local authorities, ordered the arrest of 23 prominent Sonoma County residents, including legionnaires, bankers, and the president and secretary of the Healdsburg Chamber of Commerce, on charges of kidnapping and assault. When a dozen of the men went to trial in October 1936, the courtroom was so packed even some of the defendants had to stand. The jury acquitted all parties after deliberating for 16 minutes. Business interests continued to blame outside agitators for the unrest, though Nitzberg was a Petaluma farmer and another victim was a Cotati rancher. Unionists in turn branded Sonoma County "a vigilante-infested area."

The "red purge" wasn't the only vigilante action in Sonoma County, though perhaps it was the last. The last

lynching in Sonoma County was in 1920, in the aftermath of the murder of a popular sheriff. Sonoma County Sheriff James Petray, assisted by two officers from the city, cornered three wanted members of San Francisco's Howard Street Gang in a Santa Rosa house. Shots rang out and when the dust cleared Petray and one other officer lay dead; the other died soon after. Petray's deputies nabbed "Spanish Charley" Valento, George Boyd, and Terry Fitts at the back door. Several dozen vigilantes liberated the men from the jail, took them to an isolated hillside, and hanged them. Public sympathy was solidly behind the vigilantes, and no one asked any penetrating questions. Rumors told of a party of 100 angry San Francisco policemen riding up to Santa Rosa and dispatching the thugs who had laid their comrades low. Decades later it came out that several dozen Sonoma County folks, mostly friends of Petray, carried out the lynching.

One event of the 1930s destined to have enormous impact on the Redwood Empire was the opening of the Golden Gate Bridge. People on both sides of the mile-wide Golden Gate, the opening to San Francisco Bay, had debated the building of such a span; many believed it impossible. The bridge remained in the realm of imagination until Frank Doyle, president of the Santa Rosa Chamber of Commerce, mustered North Bay supporters of a bridge at a meeting on January 13, 1923. One hundred delegates from 21 counties gathered at the Santa Rosa City Hall, and the Golden Gate Bridge Association emerged from that historic meeting. In 1930 the counties voted for $35 million in bonds to foot the bill, and construction began in 1932. On April 27, 1937, the driving of a golden rivet completed the steel-and-cement construction. Residents on both sides prepared for the party of the decade, a nine-day "Golden Gate Fiesta." On May 28, 1937, President Roosevelt pressed a button in the White House, activating the go-ahead signal at the bridge. San Francisco Mayor Angelo Rossi praised the span that "signalizes the closing, forever, of an age-old barrier to land travel." More than 31,500 cars crossed in the first 24 hours.

A special edition of the *San Francisco Examiner* announced that "the great Redwood Empire, drawn closer by the time-destroying link of the Golden Gate Bridge, scans the future with confidence and assurance in the heritage to come." The *Examiner* profiled Sonoma County, population 65,300, with its "world-famed Redwood Highway stretching away from the Golden Gate, beckoning the motorists on." The remark was a hint of traffic jams to come. The June 1 *Press Democrat* reported that at the end of Memorial Day weekend, "a solid double line of southbound cars was at a standstill as far north as Hamilton Field." Record crowds flooded Sonoma Valley and Russian River resorts, and hundreds ended up sleeping in their cars. Santa Rosans were on the hop pumping gas into an endless stream of cars. On the Fourth of July, 1937, the Russian River was a magnet for party-goers. Thousands of tourists filled the dance halls of Monte Rio and Guerneville "after traveling almost bumper to bumper across the Golden Gate Bridge and up the congested Redwood Highway," according to the *Press Democrat*. The Santa Rosa Chamber of Commerce met that week to discuss plans for a four-lane highway.

Tourists in autos were preceded by a generation that frequented Sonoma County resorts by train. After tracks were laid in the 1870s, Bay Area residents would hop on ferries and ride to Sonoma Valley or the Russian River. Farmers opened their houses and barns to boarders for the summer. Northwestern Pacific promoted North Bay hotels along its tracks in an annual "Vacationland" guidebook.

Sonoma Valley had dozens of destinations for tourists who came to hunt, fish, or "take the waters." Agua Caliente offered "the nearest hot sulphur springs to San Francisco." Boyes Hot Springs boasted 118-degree mineral baths and well-furnished tents and cottages. Northwestern Pacific's 1909 directory listed 20 hotels in Glen Ellen alone and many more in El Verano and Sonoma.

By the turn of the century, when the timber business was flagging on the lower Russian River, the tourist business was picking up steam. Sonoma County folks ran guest houses with two or three rooms, or built full-scale hotels for 100 or more. The Northwestern Pacific offered its popular "Triangle Trip" : for $2.50 passengers could ride to the Russian River on the narrow gauge in the morning, spend an idyllic day among the redwoods, and return via the broad-gauge line in the afternoon (or else do the trip in reverse).

No single event brought more business to Sonoma County than the opening of the Golden Gate Bridge, and no one worked harder than Frank Doyle to see it built. The bridge was only a dream until 1923 when Doyle, then president of the Santa Rosa Chamber of Commerce, convened a meeting to spark interest in a bridge linking the North Bay with San Francisco. On May 28, 1937, Doyle was on hand to officially open the bridge that would flood the Redwood Empire with tourists and commerce. Two months earlier, Doyle was driven across the span, making him the first person to cross the Golden Gate by automobile. Courtesy, Exchange Bank

ABOVE: *The Redwood Highway is seen as it passes through the heart of Santa Rosa's downtown business district. Courtesy, Don Silverek Photography*

OPPOSITE, TOP: *Trains were replaced by auto stages in the 1930s as the era of the railroad was surpassed by the automobile age. Courtesy, Don Silverek Photography*

OPPOSITE, BOTTOM: *Cigarettes became big business for jobbers in the 1920s and 1930s. The truck pictured here is making a delivery in the Railroad Square area of Santa Rosa. Courtesy, Don Silverek Photography*

Resorts flourished along the tracks at Mirabel, Hilton, Rio Nido, Guerneville, Guernewood Park, Monte Rio, Cazadero, Camp Meeker, and Occidental. Accommodations on the Russian River ranged from floored tents to multi-storied hotels nestled among the redwoods. Sully's Resort, for instance, sent its autobus to the Monte Rio train station to collect guests, who stayed for $20 a week in the four-story hotel or in tent cottages for a bit less. According to Sully's 1912 brochure, Monte Rio had "all the usual amusements, large dance halls, boxball alleys, moving pictures, billiards and pool," not to mention canoeing and basking on sandy beaches. The Monte Rio Hotel, showpiece of downtown Monte Rio in the 1910s and 1920s, had a unique claim to fame: each of its seven stories had a ground floor entrance. (The hotel was built against the side of a steep slope.) Hotel Rusticano in Camp Meeker advertised croquet, tennis, bowling, and dancing. M.C. "Boss" Meeker also divvied up land and sold $20 lots; for another $100 the buyer could have a cottage built. Hundreds of people bought lots from Forestville to Duncans Mills and built summer homes.

Tourism was not enough to sustain the cost of running a railroad. Timber in the Russian River area was already becoming depleted when a devastating fire in 1923 swept along the river from Guerneville all the way to the sea, destroying mills and trees. The cost of repairing aging trestles and equipment was also becoming prohibitive. By the 1920s automobiles were becoming the transportation of choice, and a new paved road linking Guerneville with the Redwood Highway was completed in 1927. Northwestern Pacific first abandoned its narrow-gauge line; as the last train pulled out of Occidental in 1930, townspeople sadly placed a banner on the train that read, "Gone, But Not Forgotten." An autobus took its place. The broad-gauge line to Guerneville saw its final run on November 14, 1935. Everyone in Guerneville took a day off and hopped on board with lunches and beer; as the train left Monte Rio for the last time, the volunteer fire department turned their sirens on full blast in farewell.

The end of the railroads to the Russian River was not the end of tourism. During the 1930s and 1940s young people flocked to Russian River resorts for nightly dances. Dance halls at Mirabel

Park, Guernewood Village, and the Grove in Guerneville booked bands to play all summer. Ray Tellier and his 15-piece orchestra played the Grove all during the '30s, and Reg Code brought his collegiate band from UC Berkeley to the Guernewood Bowl. Big bands came up to play one-night stands at Rio Nido. Ozzie Nelson's band played Rio Nido in the late '30s (Harriet was the lead singer), and the sounds of Benny Goodman's clarinet bounced off the canyon walls. There were good times as the 1930s drew to an end and the Depression loosened its grip, but in Europe and Asia, the war that would engulf the world had already begun.

In the 1930s Santa Rosa was still a small town, but Sonoma County ranked 10th in agricultural prowess among all the counties of the nation. The Sonoma County Fair was organized in 1936 to celebrate the county's produce and livestock. The first fair operated on a budget of $50,000, and charged 50 cents for admission. Courtesy, Sonoma County Library

CHAPTER SEVEN

A Toast to the Future

In 1941 Europe had been at war for two years, and the U.S. and Japan seemed headed for conflict, but on the Pacific coast, World War II caught everyone off guard. With the news of Japan's attack on Pearl Harbor on December 7, 1941, coast residents suddenly braced themselves for possible invasion. The following day army troops hurried to Tomales and Bodega Head to keep watch in hastily erected watchtowers. Ammunition was in such short supply that the man on guard duty gave his ammo to the next man coming on watch.

Troops and civilians scrambled to prepare a defense, especially after Japanese planes were spotted near San Francisco. The December 9 *Press Democrat* headline warned "Enemy Here," and Santa Rosa station KSRO shut down for several hours to prevent enemy aircraft from homing in on radio beams. Three days after Pearl Harbor, 1,200 infantrymen of the 7th Division were guarding Sonoma County from their new regimental headquarters at the county fairgrounds. Air raid wardens set up posts at strategic points like Mount Saint Helena and Mount Jackson. Attorney Red Tauzer organized 96 volunteers, mostly World War I veterans, into a unit of the state home guards in Santa Rosa. "What impressed me the most was the lack of any hysteria on the part of the men," Tauzer said. "It was a cool, clear-thinking group of American citizens."

The Santa Rosa City Council passed a blackout ordinance; one long siren blast meant "lights out." Blackout curtains went up every night all over the county. During the second blackout, on December 11, twins born to the Erwin family of Petaluma at Sonoma County Hospital were heralded as "the blackout babies."

The first tragic news came by telegram a week after Pearl Harbor. William Montgomery, a 20-year-old Navy gunner's mate from Santa Rosa, had been killed. By war's end, 243 such telegrams would come to Sonoma County homes. But there were also lucky escapes. Ensign Kenneth Eymann (later a Sonoma County Superior Court judge) was feared lost on the USS *West Virginia* at Pearl Harbor but was later found safe, away from his ship on a pass.

Wartime precautions became routine. In Bodega Bay, the Coast Guard took over the Bay Hotel and patrolled Doran and Salmon Creek beaches with dogs. Tank crews, stationed at the former CCC camp east of Freestone, regularly rolled through Bodega Bay on the way to maneuvers at Bodega Dunes. Bodega Bay became a guinea pig for camouflage experiments; longtime resident Glenice Carpenter remembers planes flying overhead and blanketing the town several times with smokescreen. Carpenter also recalls deafening sounds of a battle somewhere off Bodega Bay early in the war. The shaking from the offshore barrage was so intense that her father, who ran the Bay Hotel, hustled his customers outside. "The hotel was a rather old building, and we got out and stood in the street," Carpenter said. "We were afraid the building would fall down." The battle was never officially reported; residents suspect a Japanese submarine was intercepted near shore.

The war era brought a number of projects that would later serve peacetime uses. The airport long envisioned by county planners came to life when the Civil Aeronautics Authority provided $300,000 for a site on Laughlin Road northwest of Santa Rosa. Army interceptor squadrons practiced on the field that would later become the Sonoma County Airport. At Santa Rosa Junior College, enrollment plummeted from approximately 1,000 students to 235. But the war meant eventual expansion for SRJC. The nursing program began in 1942, and by 1943 the school housed 750 men of the Army Special Training Program. New barracks later became student housing.

While ranchers' sons were fighting in Europe and the Pacific, German soldiers were picking hops in the Russian River Valley. Camp Windsor, originally built for migrant workers during the Depression, housed 200 to 300 German prisoners, mostly captured submarine crewmen. The German POWs left their minimum security prison each morning and goosestepped out to the orchards and hop fields, singing German songs. The friendly, hard-working POWs were a big hit with local ranchers, who threw a farewell beer and pretzel party for them when the war ended.

Japanese residents of Sonoma County, most of them native born, didn't fare as well. To allay suspicions against their community, 100 members of the county's Japanese American Citizen's League met in Petaluma and drafted a statement condemning Japan for its "unprovoked attack upon the Hawaiian Islands and American possessions in the Pacific." Despite such avowals of loyalty, on February

19, 1942, President Roosevelt signed Executive Order 9066, calling for the removal of Japanese from military areas. Most of California was declared a military area, and the county's 758 Japanese residents, 550 of them born here and therefore U.S. citizens, braced themselves for relocation.

On May 11, 1942, the order came giving "all persons of Japanese ancestry" four days to sell or store their businesses and belongings. Many sold off chicks and livestock at 10 percent of market value. Homes, apple dryers, and poultry farms were hurriedly sold or leased. On May 15, with only as much clothes and bedding as they could carry, they boarded buses headed for internment camps where they would live behind barbed wire until the order was rescinded in December 1944. Most Sonoma County Japanese went to Camp Granada in Colorado. Some came home to find their businesses in good order. Others, like Sebastopol apple rancher Joe Furusho, discovered that renters had failed to keep up mortgage payments or send an agreed-upon share of profits during the war. Most of those who returned to Sonoma County recovered their farms but lost the income from their businesses for the war years. Statewide, the 110,000 imprisoned Japanese suffered a $400-million loss.

During the war Santa Rosans got a taste of filmmaking, destined to be a source of fame and income for the county. Because of wartime budget restrictions, film director Alfred Hitchcock shot his thriller *Shadow of a Doubt* on location instead of building expensive studio sets. His crew turned Santa Rosa into a movie set for a month in 1942, shooting scenes in Courthouse Square, the old Carnegie library, and the railroad depot. Hitchcock also found the perfect house on picturesque McDonald Street to serve as the home of the family in the film. "But when we came back, two weeks prior to the shooting," Hitchcock recalled, "the owner was so pleased that his house was going to be in a picture that he had had it completely repainted. So we had to go in and get his permission to paint it dirty again."

Hitchcock used crowds of townspeople as extras and also found a last-minute cast member on a Santa Rosa street corner, drafting 10-year-old Edna May Wonacott to

World War II brought a number of projects that would later serve peacetime uses. The airport, long envisioned by county planners, came to life when the Civil Aeronautics Authority provided $300,000 for a site on Laughlin Road northwest of Santa Rosa. Army interceptor squadrons practiced on the field that would later become the Sonoma County Airport. Pictured here is a pilot stationed at the airport. Courtesy, Don Silverek Photography

play the precocious young sister of the heroine. *Life* magazine was so impressed with Hitchcock's on-site shooting that it ran a photo spread in its January 25, 1943, issue, with photos of Hitch and his crew all over town. In the film, the setting was identified as Santa Rosa, playing itself: a sleepy, innocent small town, in contrast to the darker elements of the film, represented by the psychopathic uncle played by Joseph Cotten.

Hitchcock returned to Sonoma County in 1963 for *The Birds,* in which clouds of rampaging gulls and songbirds go berserk and menace the hapless residents of Bodega and Bodega Bay. The old Potter School in Bodega, now a bed and breakfast inn, played a school besieged by angry crows.

By the 1970s most films were shot on location. Sonoma County's diverse settings—coastline, vineyards, old-fashioned neighborhoods, town squares— make ideal movie sets. Teenagers in *American Graffiti* (1973) cruise down the boulevard in Petaluma. The fictional town in *Peggy Sue Got Married* (1986) features Santa Rosa High School and historic Petaluma neighborhoods. Other films shot here include *Pollyanna, Smile, The Candidate,* and *Goonies.* TV episodes are filmed here regularly, and the latest Fords and Mazdas zoom down Sonoma County highways during commercials. Playing host to film companies is a clean, lucrative industry. Like

Autumn brings brilliant hues of yellow and red to the vines of the Sonoma County wine country's 150 grape growers. The area's 11 micro-climates add variety to the county's many wine offerings. Photo by John Elk III

ABOVE: "Plant Wizard" Luther Burbank lived and worked on the grounds in Santa Rosa that today bear his name. The famous horticulturist developed more than 800 varieties of plants, including hundreds of flowers. The Luther Burbank Home and Gardens is a popular Santa Rosa tourist destination. Photo by Patty Salkeld

LEFT: A couple and their dog enjoy a lakeside picnic with several mallards at the Hop Kiln Winery in Healdsburg. Photo by Patty Salkeld

OPPOSITE: Along the placid Russian River, a stand of Monterey Cypresses is illuminated by the late afternoon sun in this view from Highway 116 near Duncans Mills. Photo by Patty Salkeld

ABOVE: Agriculture is Sonoma County's prime industry. Here, sheep graze at a farm on the Sonoma County coast. Photo by Kerrick James

OPPOSITE: Mission San Francisco Solano, founded by Padre Jose Altamira in 1823, was the last and northernmost Franciscan mission of Alta California. It is commonly known as Sonoma Mission. Photo by Patty Salkeld

ABOVE: Evoking images of early California, two young men look for a place to hitch their horses while stopping for a bite at Von Sydow's Grocery Deli on East Napa Street in Sonoma. Photo by Patty Salkeld

LEFT: A mother and child bask in the early afternoon sun on a swingset at Sonoma Plaza in the town of Sonoma. Photo by Patty Salkeld

OPPOSITE: Sonoma County's charm is due in large part to its small towns and older buildings. The Sonoma Hotel on Spain Street in the town of Sonoma typifies the area's quaintness. Photo by Patty Salkeld

The sun sets behind a sheep-grazing hill in Occidental in this serene view from Coleman Valley Road. Photo by Patty Salkeld

tourists, film crews work here, spend large amounts of money, and then go back home.

At the end of World War II, American GIs came home, ready for life to return to normal. For soldiers from rural counties like Sonoma, that meant returning to small towns. But the war set in motion forces that would transform California into the population magnet for the rest of the country. The state's two largest metropolitan areas, the Los Angeles and Bay areas, had mushroomed with wartime industry. The war in the Pacific also gave tens of thousands of soldiers and sailors a glimpse of the Golden State and its fabulous climate. Many of them grabbed their discharge papers and headed west. The state's population jumped from 6.9 million in 1940 to 10.5 million in 1950. And the numbers kept climbing; by 1990 California had nearly 30 million people.

Sonoma County missed the heavy industrialization that transformed Richmond and other cities lining San Francisco Bay. The county's population increased slowly during the war, from 69,000 to about 80,000. In 1940, Sonoma County's cities, most of them founded in the mid-nineteenth century, were still small communities surrounded by farms.

Santa Rosa had 5,220 people in 1890; in 1940 its population was still only 12,605. Petaluma was second with 8,034 people in 1940. The other cities were smaller: Healdsburg with 2,507, Sebastopol with 1,856, Cloverdale with 1,292, Sonoma with 1,158, and Cotati with 1,000. Dozens of unincorporated communities ranged anywhere from Tyrone, population 2, and Haystack, 4, to places like Geyserville, Kenwood, Forestville, and Guerneville with a few hundred each.

The advent of peacetime sparked an unprecedented building spree that spilled over into the Bay Area's rural counties. Perhaps no one is more responsible for Sonoma County's postwar growth spurt than Hugh B. Codding. A Navy Seabee during World War II, Codding came back to his hometown of Santa Rosa in 1945 with $400 and boundless ambition. By the early 1950s he had founded the community of Montgomery Village

Main Street U.S.A. has always been a focal point for the local residents of any community. This 1960s photo attests to this as locals of Santa Rosa socialize, shop, and take care of business along Santa Rosa's Fourth Street. The charm of Sonoma County has made it a favored setting for many successful films such as Peggy Sue Got Married, Goonies, American Graffiti, *and* Alfred Hitchcock's The Birds. *Courtesy, Sonoma County Museum*

(named after Bill Montgomery, the first Santa Rosan killed in the war), and built 3,000 homes, earning a reputation as the boy wonder of California construction. With *Life* photographers looking on, the flamboyant Codding built a church, steeple and all, in five hours. He later put up a house complete with shake roof and landscaping in three hours, nine minutes.

County building codes were sketchy in those days, but with the big demand for veterans housing, Codding found himself constructing homes under Federal Housing Administration rules. The FHA required steel reinforcements, a precaution Codding considered unnecessary. "Steel bars were in short supply after the war," admits Codding, "so I'd lay them out while the inspectors were there, then load them behind a jeep and drag them to the next house. Finally I wore down the ends dragging them around."

By the mid-1950s, Codding Enterprises was the largest real estate firm north of San Francisco, and Santa Rosa had 31,000 people, having annexed Codding's Montgomery Village. Santa Rosa's expansion, both in size and population, continued to outpace that of other cities in the county. In 1970, Santa Rosa had 48,000 people; by 1988 it had more than doubled to 108,700, roughly one-third of Sonoma County's population. Other towns grew more slowly. Petaluma, for instance, had 10,300 people in 1950, 25,000 in 1970, and 33,000 in 1980. Cloverdale, Sebastopol, Sonoma, Healdsburg, and Cotati remain under 10,000. But even the more rural communities saw growth of one kind or another. In Russian River communities like Guerneville, hundreds of former summer cabins became year-round homes. In the late 1960s and through the 1970s, a "back to the land" movement brought counterculture people disenchanted with the city. These latter-day utopians moved into cabins or communes like Morningstar Ranch near Occidental. The Russian River, with its relaxed attitudes, also became a mecca for gay tourists from the Bay Area in the late 1970s and throughout the 1980s. Many gays moved there permanently, adding one more element to the interesting mix of Sonoma County residents.

Despite their closeness to San Francisco and the East Bay, Sonoma County cities are not "bedroom communities." Even at the southern end of the county, only one-third of Petaluma and Sonoma Valley workers commute to neighboring counties. In Santa Rosa only 6 percent commute. With population growth came new jobs, especially when research and electronics firms discovered Sonoma

County. The biggest are Hewlett-Packard and OCLI (Optical Coating Laboratory, Inc.), which built on the fringes of Santa Rosa.

Growth also took the form of an entirely new city and a four-year college. Rohnert Park sprang up in farm country between Santa Rosa and Petaluma, and now dwarfs neighboring Cotati. Attorneys Paul Golis and Maurice Fredericks bought Fred Rohnert's 2,700-acre seed farm for $200 an acre in 1954. They drew up a master plan for a city of 30,000 with eight distinct "neighorhood units," each with 250 homes clustered around a school. Rohnert Park incorporated in 1962 and surpassed its expected 30,000 people in the 1980s.

Rohnert Park also attracted the North Bay's new state college. Sonoma State College (now University) started life in Santa Rosa in 1956, sharing a cafeteria and bookstore with SRJC. Guided by its president, Dr. Ambrose Nichols, the school moved to the Rohnert Park campus in 1966. Enrollment climbed from 274 in 1961 to more than 7,000 students in 1989.

New construction competes with agriculture for Sonoma County's one million acres. Growth is most intense along the Highway 101 corridor that stretches from Petaluma to Cloverdale. In theory, cities endorse the idea of greenbelts as buffers along the freeway, but critics of rapid growth predict that "Cloverluma," an unbroken sprawl stretching from Cloverdale to Petaluma, is fast becoming a reality as cities annex more land. By 1989 Santa Rosa was proposing to expand southward to within a half-mile of Rohnert Park. Windsor, a sleepy farming enclave of 1,000 people in 1950, will soon incorporate and rival Rohnert Park in size.

A small, planned community also popped up on the Sonoma coast. In the 1960s Oceanic Properties proposed The Sea Ranch, a posh 5,200-lot subdivision covering 11 miles of coastline north of Fort Ross. The plan galvanized the local environmental movement, which argued the development would prevent public access to a lengthy stretch of spectacular shoreline. The confrontation, with a rallying cry of "Don't Let Malibu Happen Here," helped inspire 1972's Proposition 20, which created the California Coastal Commission. The Sea Ranch controversy raged for more than a decade until the state legislature forged a compromise: The Sea Ranch construction was exempt from the control of the Coastal Commission, and the public got five access trails to the beach.

The Sea Ranch was not the first environmental battlefield. In 1963 for instance, Pacific Gas & Electric broke ground for a nuclear reactor on Bodega Head. Bodega Bay resident Rose Gaffney and her neighbors released thousands of balloons with anti-nuclear messages, to point out how far radioactive particles from the plant could travel. Their opposition helped convince PG&E to abandon the site. The only tangible reminder of the plan is "Hole in the Head," the pit PG&E dug on the mesa. It is now a pond frequented by ducks.

Sonoma County continues to capitalize on its natural assets. One resource, the Geysers, was once as famous as Yosemite is now, drawing sightseers from around the world in the 1800s. In the 1920s, steam companies tried harnessing the Geysers' power for energy, tapping the heat issuing from fissures in the county's volcanic northeastern hills. The initial scheme failed, probably because turbines and pipes of the 1920s could not withstand corrosion from the rushing steam. In the 1950s engineers took another look to determine, as one *Press Democrat* writer put it, whether the Geysers were "a useless freak of nature or cheap, limitless power." Those tests hailed geothermal energy as the miracle power source of the future.

By 1973, private companies had drilled more than 100 steam wells, selling the power to PG&E. The steam fields, located mostly within Sonoma County in the Mayacamas Mountains, became the biggest geothermal energy resource in the world, yielding enough power to supply a city the size of San Francisco. By the 1980s, however, it was clear the miracle had its limitations. Prices for steam-generated power dropped, and the subterranean steam itself was slowly being depleted.

Agriculture has been the mainstay of the county's prosperity and an avenue for new groups of immigrants. Just as Italians and Japanese came in the last century and first labored on the land, in the past few decades workers from Mexico migrated here and are a vital part of the local

Charles M. Schulz, creator of Charlie Brown, Linus, Lucy, Snoopy, and the rest of the Peanuts gang, was born in 1922 in Minneapolis, Minnesota, where he grew up playing ice hockey and sketching in the classroom. He brought his family to Sonoma County in 1958, where he continued playing ice hockey and sketching, but now it was in a rustic studio on an estate near Sebastopol. Situated on Coffee Lane, he named his new home "Coffee Grounds." Courtesy, United Media, a Scripps Howard Company

economy. There are now about 30,000 to 40,000 Hispanics in the county, concentrated in Healdsburg and Windsor.

Fishing from the county's port of Bodega Bay remains a vital industry. So are apple ranching in the west county and dairy farming in the west and south county. But if agriculture continues to flourish in Sonoma County, it will be due above all to the wine industry, with its high cash per acre yields. In 1988 wine grapes brought in $84 million of the county's $246 million in farm income. (Dairy income, the county's top agricultural money-maker until the late 1980s, was second with $62 million.) Wineries and vineyards covering 31,500 acres not only preserve

the rural character of the county, they also help draw tourists, another vital component of the Sonoma County economy.

Although some Sonoma County wineries survived the 1920s and 1930s, the post-Prohibition years did not bring a bonanza for the wine business. By the 1960s only 20 wineries remained in Sonoma County. But in the late 1960s a number of professionals, especially second-career entrepreneurs with the money to indulge a love of wine-making, began reviving wineries and experimenting with new technology. They started small wineries along the Russian River and Sonoma valleys, or resurrected neglected wineries, replacing redwood vats with gleaming stainless steel. They tinkered with new varietals. Then they began winning prizes, proving that Sonoma County wines could rival pricey European wines in quality.

In the 1970s, when Americans suddenly put down their beer mugs and discovered the glories of wine, Sonoma County vintners were ready for them. In the Sonoma Valley, entrepreneurs founded new wineries like Chateau St. Jean and revived old ones like Kenwood Winery. Wineries flourished along the Russian River, which has the majority of the county's 120-plus wineries. In western Sonoma County, growers pulled up ancient apple orchards and replanted with grapes. Suddenly winemaking was a multi-million-dollar business that attracted rich, out-of-state investors. Schlitz Brewing Company, for instance, purchased Geyser Peak in Geyserville in the 1970s.

Not all the winemakers of the 1980s are newcomers. John Foppiano came to the Russian River Valley from Genoa in 1896; today the fourth generation of the Foppiano wine dynasty sells burgundy and chablis with the appelation "Russian River Valley" on the label. The Gundlach-Bundschu Rhinefarm, after growing grapes for other wineries since Prohibition, was reborn in 1973 when Jim Bundschu, great-great-grandson of Jacob Gundlach, rebuilt the family winery near Sonoma. At the turn of the century, Samuele Sebastiani of Tuscany came to Sonoma County and took his horse-drawn wagon door to door selling wine made in a 500-gallon redwood tank. Today the third generation of Sebastianis does an international business in wines made in temperature-controlled stainless vats. Some wineries continue old traditions under new ownership. Simi Winery near Healdsburg, for instance, was founded by San Francisco wine dealers Giuseppe and Pietro Simi in 1876. Simi changed hands several times before its purchase by France's premier wine and spirits company, Moet-Hennessey.

For a while Sonoma languished as the poorer country cousin of prestigious Napa County next door. There was a time when buyers commonly asked Sonoma vintners, "Now just where in Napa is your winery?" even when the name Sonoma figured prominently on the label. Napa grapes still bring the highest prices in the state, but the price gap is narrowing, and Sonoma is pulling ahead in international recognition. Wines from two Sonoma firms, Iron Horse and Jordan vineyards, were uncorked at the 1987 U.S./Soviet summit in Washington. Only one Napa wine made the list.

In Sonoma and Napa counties, the winemaking boom dovetailed with a tourism boom. In the mid-1970s the price of gasoline suddenly soared. Vacationers from the Bay Area who were accustomed to zooming off to Lake Tahoe for the weekend looked around for destinations within an hour's drive and discovered the Russian River, the wine country, the redwoods, and the Sonoma coast.

Wineries in the northern part of Sonoma County, organized by wine publicist Millie Howie, banded together in 1974 and created the Russian River Wine Road, a self-guiding tour of wineries in the Russian River Valley. On the theory that there is strength in numbers, nine wineries pooled resources and printed a map of the wine region to lure tourists away from Napa and up Highway 101. Today the Wine Road's 50-plus wineries draw tourists whose dollars support countless restaurants, bed and breakfast inns, stores, and the wineries themselves. The counties' small towns depend heavily on tourists, and many residents feel tourism is the best of all possible industries. Visitors enjoy the woods and vineyards and go home again, leaving behind large amounts of money.

Tourism also provides an incentive to keep a naturally beautiful area as pristine as possible, despite pressures to grow. Winemaking, dairy farming, and ranching protect the county's rural appearance. The biggest challenge facing Sonoma County is the need to balance growth with the desire to preserve the county's agriculture heritage and extraordinary beauty.

Bulgarian-born sculptor Christo Javacheff built a running fence of parachute cloth in Sonoma County in September 1976. The slopes of Petaluma became an open air art gallery, with the fence originating west of Penngrove. The Christo Fence, which was 18 feet high and 24 miles long, wound its way west through the countryside and terminated at Dillon Beach, where it plunged into the sea. Christo financed the $2-million project himself and dismantled it two weeks after it was completed, distributing the poles and white nylon panels to local friends and workers. Courtesy, Don Silverek Photography

Cleveland and Schurman's hay and grain business on Third Street in Santa Rosa was the backdrop for a staff shot of Red Wagon Delivery Service's drivers and trucks in 1921. Santa Rosa's livery stables were regular customers for Cleveland and Schurman, but trucks like the ones parked here signaled the end of horses in commerce. Courtesy, Sonoma County Library

Partners in Progress

Since the days of the California gold rush, Sonoma County's hospitable climate and fertile soil have lured many settlers filled with hopes and dreams. Various types of businesses, many directly tied to the land, have thrived throughout the county.

The foothills and slopes along the eastern part of the county have been draped with vineyards since Mexican General Mariano Vallejo established the first commercial winegrowing operation in the 1850s. Mission grape stock brought to California by the early Spanish Franciscan padres provided the fruit from which Vallejo made his wine. By the mid-1850s Hungarian nobleman Agostin Haraszthy, a viticulturist who imported top-quality grape cuttings from Europe, significantly improved the quality of wine produced in eastern Sonoma County. Wine making has become Sonoma County's number one industry.

South of the vineyard-covered hills, Sonoma County flattens out into fertile flatland that stretches from east to west across the entire width of the county to the Pacific Ocean. From gold rush days to the present day, all types of livestock have grazed on the fertile, flat fields.

Water transportation along the Petaluma and Sonoma rivers, San Pablo Bay, and the Pacific Ocean permitted meat and produce to be shipped to markets in the Bay Area. During the late nineteenth century, ice cars did much to encourage growth of dairies in southern Sonoma County.

Vast stands of redwoods still cover the northern and western regions of the county. During the years of Mexican rule, Anglo settlers in western Sonoma County manufactured lumber using pit saws. By the 1850s commercial logging operations were established. The number of mills and amount of lumber produced grew rapidly during the following half-century. As redwoods in easily accessible areas became scarce, improvements in technology enabled loggers to reach deeper into more remote areas to harvest timber.

The western edge of Sonoma County snuggles up to the mighty Pacific Ocean. After serving as a route by which goods were shipped into and sent from the county for more than 100 years, the ocean now serves as a place where tourists come in search of solitude and escape from city life. The beauty of Sonoma County's rugged coastline and expansive beaches provide inspiration for writers and artists and regeneration for a growing number of people each year.

The businesses and organizations whose histories appear on the following pages have chosen to support this important literary and civic event. They illustrate the variety of ways in which individuals and their businesses have contributed to the county's growth and development. The civic involvement of Sonoma County's businesses, institutions of learning, and local government, in cooperation with its citizens, has made the area an exceptional place in which to live and work.

SONOMA COUNTY HISTORICAL SOCIETY

Today's Sonoma County Historical Society is a descendant of the Sonoma County Museum and Art Association, which was formed in 1948. The earlier group, many of whose families were Sonoma County's earliest settlers, gathered artifacts and items of historic significance but failed to ever acquire a building in which to display its collections.

In 1962 Ann Conners started a small group under the name Sonoma County Historical Society. About the same time the group was organized, Hugh Codding endeavored to set up a natural history museum. The Codding family, interested in preserving the area's heritage, donated a building on Somerville Road for use as a museum.

Saturdays and Sundays visitors could enjoy historic displays of the Sonoma County Museum and Historical Society in one part of the building and Codding's natural history museum in the other. This operation functioned well for several years but closed its doors in the early 1970s. At that point, the historic exhibits were put into storage at the Hood Mansion for approximately six years.

With the nation's bicentennial celebrations, there came a renewed interest in local history. Communities nationwide took on projects of historic preservation, the reprinting of county history books, and other efforts to commemorate local heritage.

In Santa Rosa, renewed interest in history again stirred up efforts to establish a county museum. Many locals launched a campaign to convert the old United States Post Office building on Fourth Street into a museum. At that time Santa Rosa's downtown area was undergoing redevelopment, and plans included demolition of the old post office. The campaign to save the structure succeeded, and in 1981 the old post office was moved to its present location at 401 Fifth Street. After rehabilitation, the post office reopened in 1985 as the Sonoma County Museum.

With the collections now on display in both the county museum and the Peters Museum at Santa

With the completion of the North Pacific Coast Railroad in 1876, the lower Russian River redwood forests were accessible to a waiting market. Pictured in this mid-1880s image is Brown's Canyon Trestle, south of Occidental. Courtesy, Ray Roix, Sonoma County Historical Society

Rosa Junior College, the Sonoma County Historical Society was able to direct its focus in other areas.

Over the years many small communities in the county and special interest groups have formed their own historical societies, such as the very active group that meets in Annapolis and a group that involves itself with historic railroads. The larger Sonoma County Historical Society views itself as an umbrella, supporting the efforts of the smaller groups, rather than being in competition with them.

In recent years the Sonoma County Historical Society has centered its efforts more on publications, such as its involvement in the publication of this book, than on its collections. Its approximately 500 members receive a quarterly issue of *The Journal,* which contains articles on local history. Because a great number of its members are interested in historic preservation, it has published a book on Santa Rosa's architectural heritage.

Since many of the members of Sonoma County Historical Society are also members of other historical societies within the county, the county society is able to take a broader overview of items of county-wide interest while resting assured that efforts of local interest do not go ignored.

The Sonoma County Courthouse on the Plaza in Santa Rosa, built in 1884, was the fifth of the county's courthouses and was destroyed in the 1906 earthquake. The Santa Rosa city hall building, also built in 1884, can be seen to the right of the courthouse. Courtesy, Alice Austin Hall, Sonoma County Historical Society

SONOMA STATE UNIVERSITY

Even in its early decades, a university has a profound influence in shaping the character of its community. Sonoma State University, established in 1960 as Sonoma State College and granted university status in 1978, is the North Bay region's only public four-year university. Enrollment has increased steadily, markedly in the past few years, reaching a high of 7,200 students in the fall of 1989; growth is expected to continue.

Prior to the passage of State Senator Joseph A. Rattigan's bill that established the college, the region was served by the Santa Rosa Center of San Francisco State College. The new college began instruction in 1961 in temporary quarters in Cotati under the leadership of founding president Ambrose R. Nichols, Jr. In its first year the college enrolled 265 upper-division students in programs in elementary education, psychology, and counseling.

In fall 1966 the college moved to its present campus on 220 acres of former farmland on the southeastern edge of Rohnert Park. In the ensuing years needed facilities were constructed and the grounds were landscaped extensively, including lawns, playing fields, groves of trees, and two small lakes. Recent construction has included additional student housing and a 500-seat theater building. Enrollment growth has prompted planning for an addition to the science building, a new administration/classroom building, a Student Union Building expansion, and more student apartments.

The university's academic programs, expanded and refined over the years, are based on the belief that a broad, well-balanced foundation in the liberal arts and sciences is essential for today's students. The university's undergraduate programs comprise both the traditional liberal arts and sciences and career preparation. The bachelor's degree is offered in 37 fields of study. Sixteen master's degrees and 10 education credentials are offered.

One fundamental characteristic most appreciated by visitors, faculty and staff, and especially students is the university's friendly, supportive environment. Most classes are small and emphasize hands-on, active learning, in keeping with the university's commitment to promote the open exchange of ideas and foster close interaction among students and faculty.

Sonoma State University, the 15th of the 19 California state universities, broke ground for its first buildings in the summer of 1961. The following fall 265 students were enrolled in upper-division programs. At the ceremony were (from left) Wesley Burford, campus development officer; Ambrose R. Nichols, Jr., president; Paul Golis, Rohnert Park builder; and Robert Boldoc, contractor.

Students are encouraged to become involved in all aspects of university life—study and scholarship, the social and intellectual exchanges of friendship, the arts, sports, and public service.

Educating students is and will remain Sonoma State University's primary mission. However, SSU has also reached out to the people of Sonoma County and beyond, making its rich educational and cultural resources available to all residents. It offers a wide variety of courses, lectures, and workshops, as well as performances and special events. It vigorously seeks opportunities to combine forces with local schools, businesses, and government agencies, working for the common good.

The university, which has occupied its permanent 220-acre campus since 1966, is the only public four-year university serving the North Bay region. It presently enrolls 7,200 students in undergraduate, master's, and education credential programs.

SEARS POINT INTERNATIONAL RACEWAY

Local area rancher Antonio Mattos decided in 1968 to sell a 736-acre tract for development of a raceway. The tract, which stretches out from the northern edge of San Pablo Bay, is in the southeastern corner of Sonoma County, near where the county intersects with Solano and Napa counties.

Before the end of 1968 the new corporate owner, Sears Point Investment Co., named after the longtime area family, constructed a 2.523-mile road course, a 1.949-mile short road course, and a quarter-mile drag strip. A state-of-the-art facility, it is the only true multipurpose raceway of its kind in the western United States.

Sears Point has come a long way since its beginning in 1968. The 800-acre facility is open 50 weeks per year and annually hosts major motorsports events that attract 60,000 spectators each. Many events are televised nationally, bringing tremendous exposure to Northern California as well as Sonoma County. Photo by G. Long

Actor Paul Newman's car is ready for competition at Sears Point in the SCCA Trans Am Series. Over the years many famous racers and personalities have competed on the quarter-mile drag strip and 2.523-mile road course. Photo by George Dwinell

On December 1, 1968, the Sports Car Club of America conducted a four-hour Enduro, the first event held on the new track. One of the first drivers to compete on Sears Point's twisty 2.523-mile course was an experienced driver named Larry Albedi. Today Albedi is the owner of Albedi Lincoln-Mercury in Vallejo and serves Sears Point as its chief announcer.

Sears Point was desirable as a site owing to its proximity to major highways 121 and 37. Sears Point Investment Co. built the facility to be used primarily as a raceway and operated it as such sporadically for two years, hosting such diverse events as USAC Indy-type car events and stock car competitions.

Filmways Corporation bought the track in July 1969, but soon discovered that the cost of maintaining the 736-acre facility was prohibitively expensive. For two years the track was closed, while Filmways tried unsuccessfully to find a new buyer.

In June and July 1972 Filmways permitted the San Francisco Jaycees to sponsor two events there, with profits donated toward construction of a park for children in the Hunters

Point-Bayview district of San Francisco. The two events, the Continental Prix races and the Sonoma Summersport races, were profitable enough to prompt Filmways to open the facility. Although attempts to turn a profit were never successful, Filmways built grandstand seating and hired a succession of general managers over the next five years.

In 1978 a longtime drag racer and promoter, Jack Williams, purchased the track and changed its name to Golden State International Raceway. A year later the name was changed back to Sears Point. In 1984 he sold part of the facility to real estate developer Skip Berg.

Berg not only brought much-needed financial support to Sears Point, but also a strong business management philosophy. He immediately developed plans to build auto-related industrial shop space on site. In 1985 a campaign to

The International Motor Sports Association's annual California Grand Prix has been held at Sears Point for 14 straight years. Here the 1988 race winner, number 83, Geoff Brabham, awaits the start of this prestigious event. Photo by G. Long

"Pave the Point" was launched and more than $300,000 raised to completely repave the 2.523-mile road circuit. Over the next couple of years, the track remained relatively stable. In 1986 Berg purchased Williams' remaining interest and began construction of an additional 160,000 square feet of shop space.

An interesting event occurred in 1973, when the management decided to build a banked-dirt racing oval on the property. Construction was underway with several thousands of dollars spent carving an oval out of one of the hills. One afternoon, when the oval was almost entirely finished, a grader working to level the bottom struck a natural-fed spring right in the middle of the infield of the oval. Water started pouring out of the ground, and within hours the entire oval was filled with hundreds of gallons of water. The workers barely had time to get the grader out. Now Sears Point has a perfect half-mile oval with a duck pond in the center.

During the mid-1980s Sears continued to change and grow. Ford Motor Company became a track sponsor and presently contributes to the $3 million in corporate sponsorships the track raises annually for the 50 weekends of racing it conducts each year. Racing fans have benefited from the construction of five pedestrian bridges, new grandstand seating, and additional food, concession, and souvenir gift shops. Plans for the 1991 racing season include a new media center, VIP hospitality suites, and a new state-of-the-art administration building with conference rooms, additional office space, and a restaurant on the roof.

With the spectator improvements and the variety of races held at Sears Point, it is without a doubt one of the most complete motorsports facilities in North America. It is the only track in the world to hold an NHRA (National Hot Rod Association) Winston Drag Racing event, an IMSA (International Motor Sports Association) Camel Grand Prix, and a NASCAR (National Association of Stock Car Automobile Racing) Winston Cup event during the same season (1989-1990).

During the more than 20 years Sears Point has been in operation, the facility has had an economic impact on the surrounding communities, recently in excess of $220 million annually. The impact to the Sonoma County tourist-oriented services, such as motels, hotels, restaurants, service stations, and wineries, was compiled in a recent survey study to be in excess of $197 million.

Sears Point also supports various local efforts. In 1988 alone it contributed more than $83,000 to charitable organizations, plus an additional $10,000 in tickets and season passes. It is actively involved with the Sonoma Valley Hospital Foundation, Kiwanis, the Traffic Commission of the Sonoma Chamber of Commerce, and the Sonoma County Visitors Bureau. Each year it hires 100 to 150 local youths for summer employment.

Approximately 70 businesses are located at Sears Point. One Sears Point tenant that has gained world recognition is the Bob Bondurant School of High Performance Driving. The driving school draws people from around the world to the community, and is rated one of the best schools of its type in the world.

Sears Point plans to continue to improve the spectator amenities, strengthening its claim as one of the most diverse and exciting racing facilities in the world. It will continue to attract the finest racing series in the country, as well as to develop unrelated events, such as the 1989 Sears Point charity bicycle challenge. It is proud of its position in both the Sonoma County and Northern California business communities.

A record-size crowd enjoys a beautiful California afternoon at the races. Spectators from all over Northern California flock to Sears Point for the varied major events scheduled.

JOHN TATE, INC.

On the wall beside Jean Tate's desk hang two framed patent certificates—one in English and one in Japanese. Also hanging on the wall is a full set of fencing gear. The patents testify to the inventiveness of Jean's late husband, John Tate, and the wide distribution of John Tate, Inc., equipment. The fencing gear is evidence of the spirit of Jean Tate herself, who served in Great Britain's Royal Navy and Royal Marines.

John Tate was born in Yorkshire, England, in 1924. He dreamed of becoming a mechanical engineer, but in 1942, at the age of 17, he volunteered for the Royal Navy, served in the North Atlantic and in Russian convoys, and at the end of the war found himself in Kualur Lumpur,

The late John Tate—inventor and founder of John Tate, Inc.

second in command of the Royal Malayan Navy, at the age of 21. Deciding to stay in Malaya, he joined a British oil company and traveled around Southeast Asia for the next 13 years, calling on tin mines, rubber plantations, and railroads, and taking note of what equipment could be specifically engineered to make the plants run more efficiently. He thought that he should be able to talk to customers in their

own language, so he attended school with the children to learn Mandarin and Malay.

In 1958 his company transferred him to San Francisco to open up its western division and introduce its star product, Castrol Oil. Recognizing the opportunities in California, Tate declined another promotion that would have relocated him to the head office in New Jersey, and within a short time he resigned from the company and became a manufacturers' representative for various British products engineered for agriculture and industry.

At this time John met Jean, who was not only from England but had also been in the service. Although posted to the same base and the same ship, their paths did not cross until they met in San Francisco, and in 1963 they were married. That year John Tate Company was established in Sausalito, and John Tate worked out of rented space in a large local manufacturing plant called A.G. Schoonmaker, whose owner was a friend of his. John had perceived that one of the most needed tools in the construction industry was a good quality, robust, mobile generator, powered by an air-cooled diesel engine, which he considered to be the superior power source. He designed it, sold it, and then made it with the help of a moonlighting part-time welder. The product caught on quickly, and the business grew. In 1965 the firm moved to San Rafael, where it would operate for 12 years, until the need for much larger premises brought it to Sonoma in 1977.

In 1966 the company incorporated and became John Tate, Inc.

This mid-1960s photo shows John Tate on the road to a Foster City construction site delivering four 5-kilowatt Gensets behind his Cadillac.

Demand for its products came from almost every corner of the globe, and its lines included standby generators, pump sets, a brief and unprofitable fling with a marine engine, and the Apollo Light Tower. Tate pioneered the use of the air-cooled diesel engine for agricultural use, as he was later to do for the refrigerated container, or "reefer." His design for the mobile generator incorporated an innovative idea that

Jean Tate, since 1985, has led John Tate, Inc., as chairman of the board.

Utilized during the 1981 evacuation of American hostages at the Algiers airport, the Apollo Portable Light Tower is extremely portable and durable, and raises four 1,000-watt lamps to a height of 32 feet.

he patented in 1968, that of a fuel tank contained in the frame on which the unit rested, which not only helped the unit maintain equilibrium and stability owing to its low center of gravity, but also enhanced its appearance by eliminating the usual extraneous fuel tank. This was the famous Trailertank. In 1985 he was granted a patent for a power-supply support frame for an underslung generator on a "reefer," and in 1986, eight months after his death, a patent was granted for a self-contained power supply and support for the same application. This is known as the PowerSource.

One of John Tate's favorite products was the Apollo Light Tower, a self-contained portable lighting unit that incorporates the Trailertank. Although its towing height is only five feet two inches, its telescopic boom raises four 1,000-watt metallarc lamps to a height of 32 feet, and its stabilizers enable it to withstand 100-mile-per-hour winds. In 1981 the Apollo Light Tower was seen on television news at the Algiers Airport during the evacuation of the American hostages.

The management and employees of John Tate, Inc., function cohesively. They consider themselves a tight-knit family. Like a family they share common goals about the quality of their product and share concern for each other. Also like a family the company has some highly regarded pets—in this case a small group of abandoned cats. One such cat, named Kathleen, made her home on the property from before the time Tate located in Sonoma in 1977 to the time she died in early

1989 in the executive suite.

A first-time visitor to the Tate plant is struck by several things that make it unique. The plant is clean and organized. Whereas one might expect a great deal of noise associated with production of diesel generators, the noise level is minimal. Perhaps most impressive of all is the appearance of the product. Many pieces have a baked-on enamel finish such as that on a new automobile. They look beautiful.

Jean Tate has acted as chairman of the company since her husband's death in 1985. Fred Unsworth serves as president. John Tate, Inc., employs about 40 people in its 45,000-square-foot facility lo-

cated at 21600 Eighth Street East in Sonoma. Present plans include the construction of a new facility in the mid-1990s. The company's success is proof of its slogan—"There's still a market for quality."

The company's success results largely from its ability to meet a customer's needs, and custom engineering is one of Tate's specialties. One of its most unusual projects was the incineration of liquid waste along the Alaska Pipeline. A piece of the pipeline itself stands in front of the executive offices of the company, a reminder of those exhilarating days. Flexibility leads to new products— who can say what will come in the future?

PRICE PUMP COMPANY

When the employees and customers of Price Pump Company hear the term "Pony Express," they don't think of the cross-country mail service operating in the early 1860s. They know "PONY" stands for "Parts Order Needed Yesterday," and when a parts order is stamped PONY EXPRESS, it means the order is sent out the same day it's received. But Pony Express is more than just a catchy term for a rush order, it symbolizes the firm's 57 years of commitment to customer service.

An optimistic man to begin a business in 1932, E.L. Price established his small, family-owned company in Emeryville, California. The E.L. Price Pump Company manufactured bronze gear pumps and small pedestal centrifugal pumps made of cast iron and bronze. During the 1930s and 1940s, as the firm grew, it began to focus on the manufacture of agricultural pumps. Both Sears, Roebuck and Co. and Montgomery

#1 Pump Way is home to the 31,000-square-foot headquarters of Price Pump Company.

Ward bought pumps from Price for resale in their booming catalog business.

Still a family-owned business when it moved to Sonoma in 1948, the E.L. Price Pump Company operated out of a 3,600-square-foot building, leased from Sebastiani Vineyard, on Fourth Street East. Jack Price headed the firm during the 1950s, and after his death in 1959, his wife took over the management of the company. In 1962 she sold it to Leon J. Paul, who changed the name to Price Pump Company. Although the Price family no longer owned the business, the name was retained because of the reputation for quality that was already associated with it.

During the years Price operated on Fourth Street East, cast iron gave way to stainless steel, and the company adapted to this new technology. Price Pump does more with stainless steel than any other manufacturer of the same size pumps and has developed options that improved the workability of its products.

Joe Keechlev operates the CNC four-axis horizontal machining center.

By 1967 Price Pump needed a strong administrator to chart the company's future course. Jack D. Brown, who had previous experience with Fairbanks Morse, Delavan Manufacturing Company, and FMC, was hired as the first general manager. Under Brown's leadership, the firm began to concentrate on industrial and special-purpose pumps, and reduced the percentage of agricultural pumps it manufactured.

Brown was also responsible for establishing a service that enabled Price Pump to compete with great success against other pump companies. He recognized that orders for pumps frequently involved great urgency, but the standard delivery time between order and delivery for most other pump companies was six to eight weeks. Price Pump's timetable would be different: Brown cut normal delivery time to between seven and 10 days for any product listed in the Price Pump catalogue. Today Price Pump offers three different types of shipment: standard—seven to 10 days, VIP (Very Important Pump)—next-day delivery; and PONY Express parts—same-day delivery.

By 1979 Price Pump Company had outgrown its 3,600-square-foot rented space and moved to a

Sales manager Dan McAllister (left) and general manager Gene Webb.

10,000-square-foot facility on Sonoma's Eighth Street East. Ten years later increased production necessitated the construction of a 31,000-square-foot building two miles farther down Eighth Street East—at No. 1 Pump Way.

New technology in a variety of industries has been reflected in the evolution of Price Pump's product line. Agriculture, once Price Pump's mainstay, now comprises only 7 percent of the business, but the use of liquid fertilizers and various chemicals in agriculture is generating a greater demand for Price's stainless-steel products. The majority of Price Pump's business is now done with the semiconductor, electronics, and computer industries. These companies require stainless-steel pumps for solvents and high-temperature, high-pressure ultrapure water in the production of their printed circuit boards. At least 80 percent of the liquid-cooled laser manufacturers in the United States use Price pumps to pump ultrapure water to cool the lasers for medical and industrial use.

Maintaining its emphasis on providing pumps for the new technologies, Price Pump has applied standard pump design to new pump applications and methods of manufacture. New applications include working in environmental clean-up, which is becoming a bigger part of the firm's business. Even cooking oil is filtered in deep-fat fryers with the use of Price pumps. Taking a standard pump design, the company creates and manufactures specialized pumps to serve a unique purpose.

The firm's success isn't just technological; there is the human aspect, too. This is contributed by the employees of Price Pump and their strong sense of company loyalty. Although by general pump company standards, Price Pump is small, with only 32 employees, continuity is the key to making this David successful against the Goliaths. On an average, Price Pump employees have been working with the organization for 15 years. George Block, the shop foreman, has been with Price Pump for 38 years. He has seen the company grow from about four employees to the present 32. Madeline DiGuilio, the office manager, was the only person in the front office when she began working for the company in 1965. Gene Webb began working in the shop in 1974, took four years off to complete a bachelor of science degree in 1978 at Sacramento State University, and returned to Price Pump Company, where he is now general manager.

It is not a coincidence that Price has many long-term employees. The firm places a priority on its employees enjoying their work and having fun together. One incentive to work and fun is the sales quota reward established by Paul Bargetzi, the plant manager. When a certain monthly goal is met, the company sponsors a picnic for all employees on the last Friday afternoon of the month. The entire crew can often be seen out on the field behind the plant playing riotous games of basketball and baseball, and enjoying a mouth-watering barbeque.

Today's Price Pump Company may no longer be the small, family-owned operation of E.L. Price's day, but it hasn't forgotten its roots. Sonoma is a small town and Price Pump one of its biggest employers, so the local organizations count on Price Pump's community involvement. The firm donates to local charities, sponsors a Little League team, contributes to the local high school sports and band programs, and supports the local fire department (two of the employees are also volunteer firemen). Gene Webb is a member of Kiwanis and sits on the board of trustees of the Jack D. Brown Sonoma Hospice Auxiliary, an auxiliary to support Valley of the Moon Hospice.

GLORIA FERRER CHAMPAGNE CAVES

Gloria Ferrer Champagne Caves links romantic old Spain to the modern winemaking industry in Sonoma County. The Ferrer family, owner of the champagne caves, has produced wine since the thirteenth century in the Penedes region of Spain.

For 600 years wine grapes have grown at La Freixeneda ("a place where ash trees grow"), the Ferrer estate in San Sadurni de Noya, located outside of Barcelona. In the 1930s, when Pedro Ferrer Bosch began promoting wine from his family's vineyards, he used the estate name on the label: Freixenet. Pedro developed the family business until his death during the Spanish Civil War.

Pedro's widow, Dolores Sala Vive, then took over management of Freixenet until she was succeeded by her son, Jose Ferrer Sala, in 1979. While Jose and his wife, Gloria, oversee Freixenet's extensive operations from their headquarters in Spain, their son, Pedro, and his wife, Begona, manage Gloria Ferrer Champagne Caves in the Carneros Region, southwest of Sonoma. Like its parent company, Freixenet, Gloria Ferrer is entirely owned by the Ferrer family.

Gloria Ferrer was founded in 1982 when the Carneros acreage was purchased for development of a winery. The site was chosen because of its similarity to the family lands in Spain. The soil, the sunlight, and the temperature of the Carneros area, like La Freixeneda, are conducive to growing Pinot Noir and Chardonnay grapes from which sparkling wines are made.

Jose christened the Carneros facility "Gloria Ferrer" to honor his wife and acknowledge the importance of women in the winemaking industry.

In 1986 Pedro and Begona Ferrer established their home in Sonoma. That same year the first release of Gloria Ferrer Brut Sparkling Wine won a gold medal at the Fifth Annual Atlanta International Wine Festival. The following year Gloria Ferrer Brut took a silver medal at the Orange County Fair, a gold medal at the Sonoma County Fair, and a bronze medal at the West Coast Wine Competition in Reno. It was also deemed Best of Category by *Wine Country* magazine in its annual tastings.

In June 1986 Freixenet opened the $11.5-million facility that showcases an adherence to traditional Spanish design, evidenced by its red-tile roofs, overhanging balconies, stucco walls, and arched windows and doorways.

Winemaker Robert Iantosca takes pride in his product and watches over each step carefully as it is made. After careful hand-picking, the grapes are gently

Gloria Ferrer Champagne Caves sits above land bordered by San Pablo Bay that was referred to by early Californians as "Los Carneros" after the rams that pasture there to this day. The Carneros Region is noted for its similarity to the wine country of Spain.

placed in a Wilmes membrane press, and the resulting juice is transferred to stainless-steel tanks. A special yeast culture is added, and the juice begins its first fermentation. After extensive blending experiments, the final cuvee is determined and bottled. A yeast and sugar mixture is added to the cuvee, and the second fermentation takes place in the bottle from which the sparkling wine will be eventually served. This production process, known as *methode champenoise,* is how the world's best sparkling wines are made.

The Ferrer family promotes its native Spanish Catalan culture and language in California with events that take place at the winery, such as the Catalan Food and Cultural Festival and the Catalan Christmas Dinner, or in conjunction with UC Berkeley's Catalan Studies Program. As it shares its Spanish heritage with people in the surrounding communities, Gloria Ferrer Champagne Caves provides a contemporary bond between Spain and its old colonial settlement at Sonoma.

After at least two years on the yeast, the bottles are turned and tilted daily in riddling racks until spent yeast is coaxed into the neck and removed. The bottles are then corked and rested again before shipment.

SHAMROCK MATERIALS, INC.

After World War II there came a boom in housing construction throughout California. Scores of subdivisions popped up to meet young families' demand for new homes. The increased demand for building materials in the San Francisco area resulted in shortages that delayed building projects, while contractors waited for ordered materials to be delivered.

Lee R. Ceccotti, a contractor in San Francisco and Marin counties, became impatient with the delays. In 1954 he purchased the controlling interest in Shamrock Materials, a ready-mix concrete company in Marin, in order to become his own supplier. Several years later Shamrock acquired control of Marin Masonry and began supplying brick, drainpipe, gravel, plaster, sand, rock, fireplaces, concrete, blocks, and even landscaping and ornamental products.

By 1965 Shamrock had started its own concrete trucking company—Cloverleaf Trucking, with a cloverleaf logo on each truck that made

Shamrock's mixer trucks arrived on the scene to pour concrete for the Fourth Street Mall, the downtown Santa Rosa redevelopment project begun in the early 1980s.

its link to Shamrock unmistakable. As the trucks made daily deliveries farther and farther out from the firm's headquarters in San Rafael, it became apparent that the time had arrived to open branches in other locations.

Shamrock's first Sonoma County ready-mix plant opened in 1966 on Eighth Street in the town of Sonoma. Steadily growing throughout the 1970s and 1980s, Shamrock now has branches throughout Sonoma County located approximately 10 to 15 miles apart along the Highway 101 corridor. Max Cerini, Shamrock's president, grew up in Petaluma and emphasizes local managers at all Shamrock's yards. The firm's policy also emphasizes personal service and giving equal treatment to small residential customers as well as large commercial clients.

In order to provide the best possible materials for its customers, Shamrock operates a large quality-control laboratory, which is located in Petaluma. Shamrock's quality-control lab

Shamrock Materials, Inc., with ready-mix concrete and building-material yards located throughout the North Bay, has been serving Sonoma County since the early 1960s.

is the largest in California for a supplier of its size.

Shamrock has provided materials for Kaiser Medical Center and Hospital, Memorial Hospital, Warm Springs Dam, Geysers Geothermal Power Plants, Santa Rosa Junior College, Sonoma State University, the Hewlett-Packard facility, Canine Companions, Wilfred Avenue Overpass, Sonoma County Detention Facility, Petaluma Skypark Airport, and Sonoma City Hall Plaza.

During the drought of 1981, Shamrock donated truck time, labor, and vehicles to deliver water to dairyworkers in an area near Tomales. Seven days per week, for two and one-half months, eight Shamrock employees took turns driving to the coast to deliver a load of water to a drought-stricken dairy.

Shamrock Materials, Inc., has improved its technology. For remote places such as the geysers, the company makes available portable ready-mix plants. On a nationwide level, Shamrock has marketed a computer software program that was developed by Lee Ceccotti's son, Gene, Shamrock's chief executive officer, who was a business attorney before joining Shamrock in 1978.

SERRES CORPORATION

Along the west side of Highway 12, a few miles north of the town of Sonoma, lies what appears to be a well-kept ranch with luscious green pastures enclosed by neat white-washed fences. The mailbox beside the road reads "Serres." A motorist driving Highway 12 would never guess what lies beyond the pristine setting.

The Serres ranch was part of a square-mile grant that once belonged to Fighting Joe Hooker of Civil War fame. By the 1870s the property passed to the Watriss family, and in the early 1900s it was willed to John P. Serres, grandfather of the present John P. Serres. Still standing is Hooker's ranch house, which is presently occupied by members of the Serres family. Although Serres was not linked by bloodlines to the Watriss family, the care with which he had managed the Watriss lands and ranching operation resulted in his being designated heir to the Watriss property.

In 1929 John P. Serres started a gravel-processing operation and began to sell aggregate. The business grew during the Depression, when the WPA projects generated a great demand for its products.

John P. Serres was an outgoing man who served as road master for Sonoma County, member of the election committee, fire marshall, and trustee on the local school board. Along with his work as a gravel-processing operator and his various civic responsibilities, Serres also managed to supervise the large-scale farming operation that was begun by Hooker and continued by the Watrisses.

The business took on a very different style when John's son, Frank, took over the family ranch and the gravel-processing business. Frank was less outgoing than his father. But he, too, was linked to the past by a life that started and ended in

From left to right are James Morgan, Frank Serres, and Bill Hamburg in an early 1930s photograph taken at the gravel bunkers at Serres Ranch, Agua Caliente.

the old ranch house that had been built long before by Fighting Joe Hooker. The bond between the Watriss and Serres families was passed down through successive generations. The story is told of how Frank was originally given the name John Marshall Serres. When he was still in elementary school, Frank discarded his name and chose Watriss as his middle name. From that day on, Frank was known as Franklin Watriss Serres in honor of the family that was intertwined with his own.

During the early 1950s Frank built from scratch his own rock-crushing and ready-mix plant. In addition to supplying the paving materials for other contractors,

Frank involved his own company in the heavy construction business. A significant part of Serres construction at that time involved road construction. As the number of cars in Sonoma County multiplied, there was greater and greater need for strong, smoothly paved public roads. Old timers around the Sonoma Valley have often commented, "Any road that Frank Serres built is still there." Frank was also skilled as a metal fabricator.

During the years that Frank

Serres ran the business, the company supplied concrete for several large projects, including the Hannah Boys Center and the Bank of America in Sonoma. Serres constructed new roads such as Armstrong Grove Road, Madrone Road, Arnold Drive, and London Ranch Road.

When Frank died in 1974, his son, John, the present owner, was barely 20 years old. With his arm in a cast, he took over the company. A cousin, who had recently broken a leg, helped with the start-up. John laughs when he thinks back on the two young men, who, between the two of them, only "added up to a man and a half" to run the business. Nevertheless, in spite of his youth and a temporary handicap, John managed the transition. At the present time John and his mother, the former Katherine Pedroncelli, are the corporate shareholders.

By 1974 the construction phase

The Viansa Winery in Schellville, California, recently benefited from the expert road-making ability of Serres Corporation.

of the company had slowed down in preparation to enlarge the ready-mix division. Since his father had already reduced the size of the construction crew, John was afforded the flexibility to develop the business along the lines he saw fit. John chose to increase paving. His firm presently does the majority of private work in the Sonoma area. Although the company has grown significantly during the years since 1974, most of its projects are within a 25-mile radius of Sonoma. At any given time the company has 20 to 25 jobs in progress.

Serres Corporation contributes to a variety of local efforts. It frequently donates labor and materials to projects such as the walkway that was provided for El Verano School,

the Sonoma High track reconstruction, and a parking lot that was a recent gift to the community center. Of special interest to the Serres Corporation are projects that encourage or serve the children of the area.

Perhaps one reason why John Serres takes special interest in children is because he and his wife, Judy, have two sons of their own. John Marshall Serres and his younger brother, Buchanan "Buck" Serres, are growing up on the same ranch where their father and grandfather spent their young years.

John Serres has a hands-on approach to his business. Although he employs about 50 people, he stays fully informed about all aspects of his company's business. He is confident that its size offers flexibility to vary with the economic trends. Serres Corporation looks forward to slow, steady growth as the needs of the community continue to change and increase.

GLEN ELLEN WINERY

The story of Glen Ellen Winery reads like a fairy tale set in the nineteenth century, rather than the late twentieth-century nonfiction that it is. It was 1981 when Bruno and Helen Benziger and their seven children left family and friends in New York, journeyed to California, and started a new venture that soon brought them fame and fortune. The Benziger family, with virtually no experience in winemaking, linked its future with a neglected historic vineyard located in Glen Ellen. Before eight years had passed, Glen Ellen Winery became the second-largest winery in Sonoma County and the second-largest producer of Chardonnay in the nation.

Glen Ellen Winery, 1883 London Ranch Road, is on the 100-acre parcel of land that General Mariano Vallejo gave German immigrant Julius Wegener in 1868. This tract, on the northern edge of Vallejo's 66,612-acre Petaluma Rancho, was given in appreciation for the fine carpentry work that Wegener had done for the general. Upon receiving the land, Wegener planted a vineyard and built a house that is still in use today.

After his death Wegener's land and buildings remained in his family until 1970, when they were purchased by a physician. During the first few years the doctor made improvements such as having electricity installed. He maintained the vineyards and sold the grapes to a nearby winery. However, by the late 1970s, the doctor's funds ran low. The buildings and vineyards were left unkept. Wegener's property evolved into a hippie commune.

Bruno Benziger served in the U.S. Marine Corps during World War II before returning to New York to attend college and assume a position in the family-owned Park, Benziger wine and spirit import business. In 1950 Bruno married Helen

Williamson. Their family quickly expanded as seven children—five boys and two girls— were born. For 25 years Helen and Bruno raised the brood in an 18-room house at 9 Winslow Road in White Plains.

Mike Benziger, the eldest of the seven Benziger children, left behind a large, loving family when, in June 1972, he and his future wife, Mary, set out for California just six hours after graduating from college. Benziger's education in the wine industry began as soon as he arrived in California; he got a job at Beltramo's, a Menlo Park wine shop where wine buffs congregate. For almost two years he learned about wines from wine enthusiasts, winegrowers, wine books, and wine tastings. Benziger then decided to tour the wine districts of France, Switzerland, and Germany to discover how

After a successful career as a New York wine and spirits importer, Bruno Benziger co-founded (with his son Mike) Glen Ellen Winery with the hope of retiring to the simple life of a farmer.

Glen Ellen Proprietor's Reserve wines can best be described in one word—drinkability. Quality is the hallmark of the wines offered by the Benzigers. The wines are pleasing for their enjoyable taste and their affordable price.

wineries there operated. Afterward he returned to the United States and worked in marketing for Park, Benziger in New York. After a year in sales, it was time for Benziger to return to California and learn how to make wine for himself.

In the spring of 1979 he returned to the Bay Area and found a job at Stony Ridge Winery in Livermore, where he met winemaker Bruce Rector. Rector had both an academic background in viticulture (the cultivation of grapes), which he had acquired at University of California, Davis, and hands-on experience in winemaking after working for wineries in Napa and the Monterey Peninsula. Stony Ridge was experiencing financial problems at the time, and working conditions were difficult, at best. By concentrating on blending, sometimes up to seven different wines, Rector and

ABOVE: The 100-acre Glen Ellen Estate rests in the Sonoma Valley, with vineyards planted on steep terraces in a nearly 360-degree bowl. Proximity to Sonoma Mountain and the moderating effect of the San Francisco Bay contribute to ideal growing conditions.

LEFT: Mike Benziger is pictured here doing what he enjoys most—working in the Glen Ellen Estate vineyard. His vision to produce fine Sonoma Valley wines has been a driving force behind the success of Glen Ellen Winery.

Benziger learned how to make good wine. The experience at Stony Ridge taught the two that they could produce good wine under the worst of conditions with very poor equipment.

Benziger laughs today when he remembers the 1979 harvest and his first experience with grapes. Late one night 25 tons of grapes arrived and had to be unloaded. With a light attached to his head like a miner, Benziger began unloading with a pitchfork until he was exhausted. He took a short nap and began to work again until all the grapes were unloaded. During the hectic weeks of the 1979 crush, Benziger's wife, Mary, gave birth to their first child, Erinn.

Before Mike Benziger left New York, he and his father, Bruno, had an agreement that they would invest together in a winery if Mike could locate just the right place. Throughout 1979 and early 1980, whenever they found a chance, Mike and Mary Benziger would hop into their Volkswagen and go out looking for property. They scoured California from Santa Barbara to Mendocino County before Benziger's focus settled on the Glen Ellen Ranch. After months of negotiations, the purchase was finalized on October 20, 1980. The new owners of Glen Ellen Winery were Mike and Bruno Benziger and Katherine Williamson, Mike's maternal grandmother.

Mike, Mary, and Erinn Benziger moved to Glen Ellen 11 days later. Bruno came out from New York the following January. With two children still in high school, Helen Benziger waited to move until the following summer. During the intervening months she sold the home where she had raised her children. She not only had to pack and move all the family's possessions, but also those of her mother, Katherine Williamson, who moved to California with them. Finally, on June 29, 1981, Helen and her two youngest children, Chris and Kathy, and Williamson all arrived in California.

Seven days later, on July 5, 1981, ground was broken for the new 6,500-square-foot winery. Dale Chaffin was hired as the carpenter with the Benzigers serving under him as laborers. Jerry, the fourth Benziger son, did a large part of the initial construction and worked on later additions.

The crush that began in August 1981 took place under very primitive conditions. The winery still had no roof. Without any stainless-steel tanks, the grapes were pitchforked into two milk trucks where they fermented. The Sauvignon Blanc, Cabernet Sauvignon, and Chardonnay grapes were bottled using home wine-making bottling equipment. Winemaker Bruce Rector was hired as a consultant.

The wine-producing operations at Glen Ellen picked up speed in 1982 with the production and broad distribution of varietals (wine named after the principal grape from which it is made). Bruno hired a wine broker in San Francisco and then went on the road himself. Bruno traveled the country marketing varietals. In a low-key fashion he asked distributors if they would display his product. He promised to return and pick up whatever did not sell. Varietals at the price Benziger was offering them were unknown at that time, but the market was ready. Bruno achieved instant distribution for Glen Ellen's Proprietor's Reserve wines. That same year Glen Ellen won the Sweepstakes Award at the Sonoma County Harvest Fair for its estate-grown (wine made from grapes grown on the Glen Ellen estate) Sauvignon Blanc.

When they started the winery, the Benzigers set a goal of selling 55,000 cases by 1990. Sales rapidly increased from the 2,000 to 3,000 cases of estate wines sold in 1981. The second year sales rose to 6,200 cases. In 1983 sales jumped to 43,000 cases, and up to 140,000 cases in 1984. In 1985 and 1986 cases sold equalled 380,000 and 780,000, respectively. Production passed the one-million mark in 1987 with 1.6 million cases, which increased to 2.4 million in 1988. Sales for 1989 have risen to 2.7 million cases with gross revenues of nearly $75 million.

Growing at an average annual rate of 247 percent has brought major changes in the overall operation of the winery. Whereas the 1981

As the "chief emotional officer" at Glen Ellen, Helen Benziger provides the support that holds the winery together, whether she is entertaining dignitaries, cooking lunch for employees, or playing grandmother to her 11 grandchildren.

crush took place in an unfinished winery, by 1989 the crush took place at eight different locations statewide, each with a winemaker on site. The little bottling line that the family operated by hand in 1981 was replaced two years later by a semi-automatic bottling line and again in 1986 by a still larger bottling line. Glen Ellen's few employees of 1981 had grown to 15 by 1986. By 1989 the number had risen to 170 people with more being hired all the time. The winery is in operation 18 hours per day, six days per week.

On June 28, 1988, Glen Ellen Winery began operation at Carneros. That facility handles exclusively the Proprietor's Reserve and M.G. Vallejo lines. The plant at Glen Ellen bottles only the super-premium wine, originally known as Glen Ellen White Label, but renamed Benziger of Glen Ellen in 1988.

Mike and Joe Benziger and Bruce Rector are in charge of production; they oversee every aspect of production from the growing of the grapes until the bottled wine is loaded onto trucks.

They approach wine blending in the same fashion that a cook would approach a shelf of ingredients—with an eye to how each addition adds flavor and balance. Glen Ellen views its wine as a part of the meal that enhances and complements the total dinner. This approach requires that the winemakers keep themselves attuned to changing tastes in food.

Bruno, Bob, Jerry, and Chris Benziger focused their efforts on marketing and sales. The marketing astuteness that Bruno developed dur-

Glen Ellen cellarmaster, Joe Benziger, is pictured here tasting tank samples, part of the constant process of monitoring the maturation of each individual wine. Joe, his brother Mike, and Bruce Rector make up Glen Ellen's winemaking team.

ing his years at Park, Benziger has been a significant asset in the success of Glen Ellen. During the 1980s Bruno was at the helm while Bob managed national sales, Jerry headed eastern sales, and Chris took over marketing the super-premium wine, Benziger of Glen Ellen. Bruno directed overall marketing until his unexpected death in July 1989.

One of Bruno Benziger's most successful decisions pertained to the Proprietor's Reserve label. He zeroed in on the gap that existed between jug and premium wines and filled it with his remarkably successful, low-cost, high-quality wine. Although using the name Proprietor's Reserve on a label has traditionally identified the wine as a winery's limited-release wine, Benziger broke with tradition and used the term on his best-selling, popularly priced wine.

Her title of director of hospitality understates Helen's function at the winery. She provides the warmth and optimism necessary for

Glen Ellen Winery was founded in 1980, but the vineyards date back to the 1860s. Shown here is the winery home Julius Wegener built for himself in 1868 (he was M.G. Vallejo's carpenter). Bruno and Helen lived at this residence until recently.

smooth operations when so many family members work in such close proximity. She has given all of her children the security required for them to laugh at themselves and see the humor in their lives. Likewise she has taught them to respect one another and to function as a team with each doing his or her best to contribute to the overall operation. She has the special gift of knowing how to make a visitor feel like one of the family. She dishes out encouragement with one hand and lightheartedness with the other.

Patsy, the elder of the two Benziger daughters, is married to Tim Wallace. Patsy remained in New York and pursued a career in nursing until 1988, when she and her family moved to Glen Ellen. Patsy has been gathering the archival resources for the winery. Her husband, Tim, with a graduate degree from Harvard School of Business, is the winery's director of marketing and became a partner in 1988.

Mike, Bob, Joe, and Jerry each has a supportive wife. Mike's wife, Mary, has been a key player from the days of Beltramo's and Stony Ridge up through the years of turning an unkept vineyard into a thriving economic success. When Joe was needed at Glen Ellen, he and his wife, Diane, moved from New York to California when their first child, Kelly, was but two months old. Benziger grandchildren, especially the older ones such as Erinn, Buck, and Kelly, are at home around the winery.

Two of the general partners at Glen Ellen Winery are not members of the Benziger family. They are Bruce Rector, enologist (scientist of winemaking), and Mark Stornetta, chief financial officer. Rector served Glen Ellen Winery as a consultant for four years then came on board full time in 1985 and was made a general partner.

Stornetta studied agricultural business management and agricultural economics at Cal Poly, San Luis Obispo, and University of California, Davis. In 1981, when Stornetta was with the Sonoma Valley branch of the Production Credit Association, he became acquainted with Bruno Benziger, who was then involved with establishing the winery. In 1986, when the winery's phenomenal growth demanded a full-time experienced financial officer, the Benzigers entrusted that part of the operation to Stornetta.

Mike Benziger uses the word "magic" when he discusses why people choose Glen Ellen wine over other brands. "The thing we got going from the beginning, the thing that most marketers dream about, was that our product has a personality that people can identify and empathize with. They remember the story behind it. They can come up and see a family. There's a place for them to touch and see. They never forget it. If you can reach that, you're the luckiest guy in the world. If you can reach that, you've got the magic."

Visitors come to Glen Ellen, taste the wine, and walk among the old buildings. They meet Benzigers in the tasting room and see them dashing about doing their jobs. Goober, the large chocolate-brown Benziger dog, may lumber over with a stick in his mouth—a welcoming present. A visitor remembers this whole scene when he reaches for a bottle of wine on a store shelf. It is the Benziger family itself that is Glen Ellen Winery's best blend.

Glen Ellen Winery's energy and success are purely a case of family pride. Bruno, Helen, and the families of the seven children have worked tirelessly to fuel the realization of their dream.

HUNT AND BEHRENS FEED MILL

It is hard to pass through Petaluma without taking note of the tall Hunt and Behrens Feed Mill that stands high above 30 Lakeville Street on the Petaluma River just north of Washington Street. As prominent as this mill has been for almost a half-century on the Petaluma landscape, its history can be traced to a different location.

In September 1921, when the Petaluma River served as the principal transportation route for goods going back and forth from San Francisco to north-central California, Marvin L. Hunt and Carl N. Behrens took advantage of an available site upon which to construct their mill. The first Hunt and Behrens Feed Mill was located at the corner of First and C streets, where barges arriving from San Francisco Bay had to make their turn-around to begin their return trip.

The two men had experience working at George P. McNear's mill

First and C Street was home to Hunt and Behrens Feed Mill from 1921 to 1945. The Petaluma River location allowed barge shipment to and from San Francisco with road and railway access to points beyond.

and were inspired by the changes they saw taking place in the animal feed industry. New discoveries were being made concerning the role of vitamins, minerals, proteins, and energy in animal nutrition. Previously, animals that produced meat, milk, and eggs had been fed grains, mill feeds, hay, grass, and pasture. The 1920s ushered in formula feeding as a common practice. During those years many of the flour mills in Petaluma were converted to animal feed mills.

Drawing on their past experience, Hunt and Behrens recognized the need for better feeding rations and improved feeding programs. The two men set up an operation that was dedicated to two primary

goals—individual service to their customers and efficiency in production to keep costs low. By keeping their focus on these two goals, Hunt and Behrens kept pace with the innovative changes that occurred during the 1920s and 1930s. Over the years many other feed mills were established and then eventually closed their doors. Hunt and Behrens mill prospered because it offered consistency in its service and the quality of its product.

Just prior to World War II, Hunt and Behrens began construction of a new mill at 30 Lakeville Street, Petaluma. The mill was completed shortly after the war ended. The new facility housed the office, retail store, mill warehouse, shops, garage, and storage all in one location for forklift operation.

In 1947 Marvin Hunt sold his interest to Carl Behrens, who made partners of his son, Ed, and his son-in-law, Earl Egan. In the first few

Hunt and Behrens has grown with Petaluma's great agricultural tradition since the 1920s. In this photograph the town advertises "The World's Largest Egg Basket" on a float in the Butter and Eggs Day celebrations, held from the 1920s to the 1940s.

years after the war, the mill took on several new employees, eight of whom would eventually also become owners of the Hunt and Behrens Feed Mill. They were Joe DeCarli, Bob and Spirito Falco, Bill DeMorales, John Rollage, Joe Masciorini, Al Bonomi, and Ben Barri.

"Ranchers Mixtures a Specialty" has been a motto at Hunt and Behrens since Carl Behrens initiated a program to provide individualized feed for each customer on each delivery. This specialized service was unique to the Hunt and Behrens mill. It was the practice to make one mix for each type of feeding program—one dairy feed, one poultry feed, etc. Carl Behrens' innovative concept has provided excellent service to its customers to the present time.

Spacious facilities at the modern mill permitted Hunt and Behrens to initiate the first bulk delivery of mixed feeds. This, like other changes and improvements, has been continued by the owners over the years. The primary focus of providing the best feed at the least cost has remained unchanged. When

feed that had previously been delivered in sacks could be more economically delivered in bulk, the mill helped its customers build bunkers, bins, and tanks on the ranch.

Over the years the mill has maintained its specialized service to customers with individualized needs. Feed is available to all types of ranchers—those who raise turkeys, steers, horses, swine, rabbits, dairy cows, lambs, sheep, ducks, and poultry. One of Hunt and Behrens' customers is the Reichardt Duck Farm, which raises Peking Duck for Bay Area restaurants. Not only do Hunt and Behrens deliver feed for customers from the coast to Nevada, but one customer from as far as Hong Kong orders concentrated feed to provide high-quality, low-cost nutrition for animals in his country.

Just as Hunt and Behrens has incorporated new, more efficient methods in its production, so it has also had to expand its plant when necessary and groom new owners when older ones want to retire. To meet the increasing needs for a larger facility, both the storage and milling capacities of the mill were doubled in

the 1950s. Then, in the 1970s, a second mill was constructed at the same location as the mill built in the 1940s. The purpose of the second mill was to maintain efficiency by conducting all operations under one roof while allowing the flexibility of operating the poultry feed division separately from the dairy feed division. In the mid-1980s an additional batching station was added for dairy feeds.

It has been a successful practice to have sons of owners and customers take the responsibility and authority to manage each department of the business. At Hunt and Behrens, most of the present owners are sons of prior owners or customers. Within recent years Joe Masciorini, Jr., Bob Falco, Mike DeMorales, and Dan Figone have bought into the business.

All at Hunt and Behrens Feed Mill acknowledge that today there is a greater need for low-cost feeding programs to keep the price of milk, eggs, and meat as low as possible. All derive pleasure from meeting the daily challenges of their jobs and thank all the customers for Hunt and Behrens' success.

Its original four acres doubling twice since 1945, Hunt and Behrens' new milling facilities on Lakeville Street in Petaluma include warehouses, garages, an office, and a maintenance shop.

BERRY'S SAWMILL, INC.

Heavy vegetation conceals an expansive lumberyard and sawmill that sit just a few yards off heavily traveled Highway 116 between Guerneville and Duncans Mills. The sign along the highway marking the entrance to the mill gives no indication as to the vastness of the operation that spreads out over 30 acres.

The Berry family's tie to the land dates back to 1888, when owner Loren Berry's maternal grandfather, George Montgomery, bought 1,200 acres in Cazadero from Silas Ingram. Although the family continued to own the land, Montgomery made his primary home in Oakland. It was not until 1926, after Montgomery's daughter, Faith, had married Merrill Berry, that the family established its residence in Cazadero.

Although Merrill Berry was from a ranching background, he and his son Loren began harvesting timber in 1939. They had difficulty finding a market for their logs. The following year they set up a sawmill.

The site of Berry's first mill was alongside the main street of Cazadero where the North Western Pacific Railroad station had once stood. To keep logs soft and free of debris, Loren bulldozed an area nearby where logs were ponded prior to being milled. Berry's innovative use of band saws conserved both timber and power. From the outset the mill specialized in oversize timbers.

Government regulations aimed at cleaning up the environment have fallen heavily on the lumber industry since the 1960s. Disposal of by-products—bark, sawdust, chips, and shavings—has become an important part of Berry's overall operation. Berry addressed the problem of noise by constructing a 180-foot-long room along one side of the

This 1947 photo shows Berry's Sawmill in Cazadero six years after its beginning. The large building housed the band saw, edger, and trim saw. The multipurpose derrick can be seen at right.

mill to help buffer any noise that might disturb the surrounding neighbors. Berry's sense of responsibility to the neighbors who might be negatively impacted by negligent mill operations is apparent when Loren's son, Jim, speaks about the multitude of government regulations. Jim comments, "They [the regulations] make us do a better job."

The Berrys believe that producing 40,000 board feet of lumber (half redwood, half Douglas fir) per day is only a part of their job. Loren and his son Bruce also serve as directors for a nonprofit, interdenominational retreat facility started by George Montgomery in Oakland. For 35 years Loren has been a supporter of a Christian camp located seven miles from the mill. The Berrys donate their time to manage timberlands for various camps. They believe that as stewards of the land they must involve themselves in fire prevention and land conservation.

Each week groups of schoolchildren from all over California visit Berry's Sawmill, Inc. Loren enjoys leading the children on a tour and teaching them about tree regeneration. He points out that many of today's forests are comprised of healthier trees than were the overgrown forests of the past.

Today 40,000 board feet of redwood and Douglas fir are produced daily by Berry's Sawmill, Inc.

THE GREAT PETALUMA MILL AND STEAMER GOLD LANDING

The Great Petaluma Mill, which now houses 21 specialty shops and restaurants, including the restaurant known as The Steamer Gold Landing, has repeatedly adapted to the evolving economic base of the town of Petaluma. Only the farsighted vision of a developer saved The Great Petaluma Mill from demolition in 1975.

Several nineteenth-century buildings, mostly warehouses and sheds, were incorporated into the massive grain mill that George McNear built in 1902 to supply feed for the growing poultry industry. Oriented toward the Petaluma River from which it shipped its grain, McNear's mill was constructed at the foot of B Street. Evidence of the earlier buildings can be seen along B Street in the thick stone walls built in 1854 as part of the Baylis warehouse. The stone walls are joined by McNear's 1902 concrete addition.

The George P. McNear Company continued to operate the Great Petaluma Mill until 1959, when it was bought out by a competitor, the Golden Eagle Milling Company. Golden Eagle moved into the building vacated by McNear, until it too shut down operations after about 10 years, when the chicken industry moved away from Petaluma. The building sat empty and was scheduled for demolition.

In 1975 a developer recognized

George P. McNear's 1902 grain mill now houses 21 specialty shops and restaurants. McNear incorporated several former warehouses and sheds into his large mill building. The stone wall of a warehouse built in 1854 can be seen on the B Street side.

the retail possibilities offered by such a large historic structure. He divided the massive interior into several shops and left a large open area for a restaurant.

In the late 1970s Ned Foley, a Southern Californian with restaurant experience, stepped forward to construct and manage the restaurant. Massive hewn timbers and rustic masonry walls of the area where grain was once stored make up the walls of Steamer Gold Landing. Drawing on the history of Petaluma for the theme of his restaurant, he gave

it the name in honor of the Steamer Gold paddleboats that once transported passengers and freight between San Francisco and Petaluma. The actual historic landing was located on the turning basin, across the Petaluma River from McNear's Mill.

The Great Petaluma Mill is a part of Petaluma's Main Street Project, an historic preservation effort to revitalize the downtown area and focus on the historic qualities unique to Petaluma. The mill's general manager, Chuck Offerman, is proud of the mill's link to Petaluma's heritage.

To draw public attention to Petaluma's old downtown area and the turning basin, the mill hosts the Petaluma River Festival each August. The festival draws about 20,000 people to the Petaluma River Turning Basin. Visitors enjoy music, arts and crafts, boat rides, and various forms of entertainment. Proceeds from the festival are used to enhance the turning basin.

The Great Petaluma Mill and Steamer Gold Landing are helping to chart a future for Petaluma built upon the uniqueness of the past.

Completely revitalized, the Great Petaluma Mill has renewed the waterfront and has become a mecca for Sonoma County shoppers.

THE SEA RANCH

For hundreds of years before Europeans ever saw the northern Sonoma coast, the gentle Pomo Indians made seasonal treks to the coast to hunt, fish, and gather foodstuffs. Occasionally today a hiker on these grounds will come upon a broken obsidian arrowhead or evidence of an ancient midden (refuse heap).

The Indians' way of life came to an end in 1846, when the Mexican governor gave the land to a German as part of a land grant. For the next century cattle and then sheep grazed the gently sloping marine terraces. Early in the 1900s the ranch acquired the name Rancho Del Mar. Today the Black Point barn, at the south end of The Sea Ranch, and the Knipp and Stengel Ranch barn, which sits alongside Highway One five miles farther north, stand as reminders of the ranching days on The Sea Ranch, a planned rural community.

Timberlands were extensively logged, and sawmills sprang up along the northern Sonoma coast in the late 1800s. The small, whitewashed Del Mar School, which was built for the mill workers' children in 1905, stands next to the highway near the north end of the ranch.

In 1964 Hawaii-based Castle & Cooke purchased the 5,000-acre Rancho Del Mar to develop as a second-home community. The firm sent architect and planner Al Boeke, who began to conceptualize the possibilities of a development that harmonized with and was not injurious to the environment.

Assuming the role as steward of the environment, the company hired experts who studied all segments of the ecology—marine animals, land formation, climate, wind directions, and native vegetation. Landscape architect Lawrence Halprin oversaw landscape and site planning; architect Joe Esherick designed hedgerow homes. The architectural firm of MTLW (Charles Moore, William Turnbull, Donlyn Lyndon, and Richard Whitaker) created the unique Sea Ranch design with Condominium I and many of the early homes.

Planners formulated a set of building design guidelines that required that structures would blend into their natural setting. Sea Ranch architecture is renowned for being environmentally sensitive. The name given the development reflects a continuity and respect for the past, as Rancho Del Mar has been simply translated into its English equivalent—The Sea Ranch.

The aim of the developers was to create a place where people could come to escape the rigors of city life. Those seeking solitude can walk the long stretches of sandy beaches, hike along miles of trails, or simply do nothing but watch the whales migrate along the coast from November through April. Other activities include swimming, tennis, golf on The Sea Ranch Golf Links, or a picnic at the Hot Spot on the Gualala River.

Visitors usually make their first stop at Sea Ranch Lodge, which houses a store, post office, real estate office, restaurant, a fireside room, and guest accommodations. Sea Ranch Village Inc. (a partnership of Sea Ranch owners), which purchased the property in 1988, has contracted with most of the original architects to design a small village center with an expanded lodge and small conference facility for the ever-increasing number of people who come seeking escape.

Offering a place of retreat from the rigors of urban life, The Sea Ranch features a coastal paradise with quiet beaches and miles of hiking trails.

The nine miles of beaches surrounding The Sea Ranch are breathtakingly beautiful; hours may be spent exploring the tidepools or watching the sea lions play offshore. The gray whale migration, observable from November through January, is an exciting and powerful testimony of nature awaiting Sea Ranch guests.

KAISER PERMANENTE MEDICAL CENTER

Kaiser Permanente's roots go back to the 1933 Los Angeles Aqueduct project in the Mojave Desert. To provide health care for industrial workers on that construction project, Dr. Sidney Garfield established a hospital, where physicians initially worked on a fee-for-service basis. This arrangement was eventually changed to a prepayment plan.

Dr. Garfield and the workers found this to be a highly satisfactory arrangement for physicians and workers alike. The workers gained financially when health and safety measures were initiated to minimize worksite injuries.

News of Garfield's health plan reached Edgar F. Kaiser, who requested a similar plan for Kaiser workers and their families at the Grand Coulee Dam worksite. When Garfield again succeeded in meeting medical needs while keeping costs reasonable, Kaiser engaged him to organize plans for workers at shipyards during World War II. The plan was offered to other employers as well. By 1945 there were 25,000 members. By the end of 1989 more than 6 million people were voluntarily enrolled in the program in 17 states.

Kaiser opened its first medical of-

The Kaiser Permanente Medical Center in Santa Rosa serves more than 80,000 health plan members in Sonoma County. The new hospital, which opened in 1990, features all basic medical services, including 24-hour emergency care.

fice in Sonoma County in leased space in 1980. The following year the program unveiled its own medical office at the corner of Mendocino Avenue and Bicentennial Way in Santa Rosa. A second medical office opened in 1987.

Kaiser's new 106-bed, full-service hospital began accepting patients in early 1990. The 160,000-square-foot facility features four surgery suites, seven labor-delivery-recovery suites, a newborn nursery, and a 24-hour emergency department.

The $45-million hospital also headlines a computerized Patient Care Management System to help manage patient care and information and to schedule tests via computer terminals. This will save staff time and reduce the chance for error.

Approximately 900 health care workers at the medical center provide inpatient and outpatient medical care for more than 80,000 voluntarily enrolled health plan members in Sonoma County.

Kaiser Permanente prides itself on providing high-quality, cost-effective health care. Along with medical care for illness and injury, preventive measures are also stressed. Members and nonmembers can attend an array of health education classes.

A health education center is now open to the public. Staff members assist visitors in locating information on cholesterol, parenting, diabetes, and more. The center features videotapes, audiocassettes, reference books, and books for sale.

Kaiser also takes health education into local schools. A traveling troupe of professional actors visit elementary schools with a live musical. "Professor Bodywise" helps teach kindergarten through sixth-graders the basics of good health and nutrition. A second educational program about AIDS, "Secrets," is geared for junior high and high school students.

Another aspect of Kaiser Permanente's community involvement is grants and donations to local nonprofit agencies. In 1989 the medical center awarded more than $20,000 in grants and donations to charitable agencies in Sonoma County.

RED LION HOTEL

In 1959, when Tod E. McClaskey, co-founder of the Thunderbird Coliseum Motor Inn in Portland, Oregon, was making his plans to open his first motor inn, he was confronted by pessimistic predictions about his financial future. Fortunately, the predictions failed to come true, and within a few years several Thunderbird Motor Inns were built in the West. McClaskey's commitment to quality was reassuring to travelers who visited the Thunderbird Motor Inns. When the chain was renamed Red Lion Inns, the reputation for quality continued to attract guests.

According to general manager Tim Bridwell, in the mid-1980s a land developer, Jimmy Rogers, and the city of Rohnert Park teamed together to decide how a large parcel of land then for sale might best be utilized. Both Rogers and the city decided that the parcel would be an excellent location for a hotel development.

Red Lion Inns already dot the north-south corridor along I-5 from Seattle down to Ontario, California. Recently, its focus has been California's coast corridor, with a string of hotels that stretches from Eureka down to Costa Mesa. It has directed more of its development to hub areas that surround large cities and are served by major airports. Red Lion has become a strong competitor in an upscale market.

With encouragement from Rohnert Park, Red Lion Inns and Blount Development Company of Montgomery, Alabama, teamed together. Red Lion was enthusiastic about the location, and Blount was ready to get into the hotel industry. Feasibility studies by Pannell, Kerr, Forster were encouraging, and the team decided to proceed with construction.

The Rohnert Park location offered easy freeway access and the

The Rohnert Park Red Lion Hotel serves the local community, tourists, and business travelers with its easy accessibility, central Sonoma County location, and numerous facilities.

amenity of a golf course. The Red Lion properties in the surrounding areas—Eureka, Redding, Sacramento, and San Jose—meant that the degree of familiarity would already be high. The city itself did everything possible to facilitate the project. Bridwell has only complimentary words about the assistance provided by Rohnert Park. With cooperation from all sides, the construction phase of the project was completed three months ahead of schedule. The hotel was built on six and one-half acres by Blount Brothers Construction.

The Rohnert Park Red Lion Inn serves the local community in several ways. It provides a tax benefit to the city. Its easy accessibility, central county location, and numerous facilities make it a popular local gathering place. As a large upscale facility that can be reached in a short time from any place in the Bay Area, it draws to Sonoma County conventions and other gatherings, thereby bringing in retail dollars that otherwise would go elsewhere.

SONOMA COUNTY MUSEUM

The impressive structure, which now houses the Sonoma County Museum at 425 Seventh Street in Santa Rosa, functioned differently in the daily lives of earlier Sonoma County citizens. From 1910 to 1966 it served as the United States Government Post Office and Federal Building. Originally constructed at 401 Fifth Street, the building, known as a fine example of classic federal architecture, was designed by the nationally renowned architect James Knox Taylor.

In 1979, when downtown development became a threat to the structure's existence, the building was moved from its original location. The local community paved the way for its opening in January 1985 as the Sonoma County Museum, a showcase of Sonoma County history, art, and heritage.

Walking up the wide granite steps and passing between massive columns, visitors enter a lobby of ornately designed plaster walls and finely carved woodwork. To the west, a fine old oak stairway winds its way to the second floor. The grand entrance hall, with its marble terrazzo floor and chandeliered ceiling, impresses the visitor.

This lively museum's primary role is the preservation and presentation of Sonoma County's cultural heritage. The museum's temporary exhibits appeal to a variety of interests and are enhanced by programs, demonstrations, and related participatory activities.

The museum has an oral history program that not only collects the personal reminiscences of old-timers, but also records detailed information on specialized subjects from locals who are themselves a valuable cultural resource.

The museum offers a special outreach program to schools. Museum volunteers take historic items that are of special interest to schoolchildren. The volunteers tell the children about the items and answer the children's questions. The goal of the pro-

The 1910 old post office building has been rehabilitated and now houses the collections of the Sonoma County Museum, used for many exciting temporary exhibits.

gram is to help children develop pride in their heritage.

Seeing themselves as stewards of Sonoma County's history and arts, museum director John Lofgren, curator Eric Nelson, and administrative secretary Judith Glas are generous in their praise of volunteers whose help is essential for the museum to function.

The Sonoma County Museum is partially supported by a large and growing membership. It hosts various fund-raisers, such as art auctions and wine and beer tastings. The volunteers operate a gift shop in the lobby that sells books of historical interest and related items.

Much work was required between the time the old post office building was moved to Seventh Street and the day it opened as the Sonoma County Museum in January 1985.

HOLIDAY INN—SONOMA COUNTY WINE COUNTRY

In the mid-1980s the owners of Fountainhead Inn, at 3345 Santa Rosa Avenue in Santa Rosa, decided that they needed to have a name that was familiar to the public in order to capture more of the rapidly increasing Sonoma County tourist market. They contacted the Holiday Inn corporate headquarters to find out what was involved with acquiring a franchise to operate a Holiday Inn. After various required improvements were completed, the facility opened in September 1986 under a new name: Holiday Inn—Sonoma County Wine Country.

During the 1980s many Sonoma County wineries were opening tasting rooms to the public and attracting greater numbers of tourists each year. That led to the need for a greater number of lodging accommodations. The most influential reason for placing a Holiday Inn at this particular location was its proximity to so many wineries.

The Holiday Inn includes 104 guest rooms, a restaurant with seating for 75, and a small lounge. In order to meet the needs of visitors who are concerned with physical fitness, the Holiday Inn features a 13,000-square-foot health spa, which includes a weight room, an area for aerobics classes, a pool where classes are conducted, a clothing boutique, and a beauty salon. Guests can relax in a Jacuzzi or enjoy a massage.

Outdoor recreation activities are also offered to guests of Holiday Inn. In addition to a swimming pool, there are two tennis courts and a small putting green.

The owners of Holiday Inn

The Holiday Inn—Sonoma County Wine Country greets tourists who are weary after a day visiting the local wineries.

know many travelers are brand loyal; after a day out on the road, travelers will seek out a Holiday Inn because they can be assured of comfortable accommodations. The new Holiday Inn in Santa Rosa is easily accessible from Highway 101. It is situated to the east of the highway, between the Hearn and Todd Road turnoffs.

Holiday Inn also sees itself serving the relatively new, but rapidly growing market of tourists who enjoy visiting wineries in various locations around the United States. An organization that sponsors wine tour packages has contracted to use Holiday Inns exclusively for its tours of winemaking areas.

The Holiday Inn offers a 3,800-square-foot meeting space that is available for banquets, weddings, and seminars. The inn is a member of both the San Francisco and Sonoma County Convention and Visitors' Bureaus. Holiday Inn serves the local community by providing support to all nonprofit organizations.

As greater numbers of the traveling public are drawn to the beautiful Sonoma County wine country, Holiday Inn—Sonoma County Wine Country anticipates welcoming tired tourists after a day of touring the wineries.

Facilities for banquets, weddings, and seminars are available at the Holiday Inn.

KFTY-TELEVISION CHANNEL 50

Located in the heart of Santa Rosa at 533 Mendocino Avenue is a modern building bearing a supergraphic "50." The building houses the offices and studios of KFTY Television Channel 50, owned and operated by Sonoma Broadcasting, Inc. Since 1981, when the station first went on the air, it has been the only television station in the North Bay.

As the first commercial independent broadcast station north of the Golden Gate, KFTY-TV gave North Bay businesses the opportunity to incorporate television advertising into their marketing plans. And unlike most television advertisers who rely on production companies to provide commercials, KFTY advertisers worked directly with KFTY Productions to develop their on-air message. KFTY Productions now averages 1,000 new commercials per year.

KFTY Productions has expanded its sales and services to include nonbroadcast videotape presentations for promotional and educational purposes. In 1984 KFTY produced videos for the Sonoma County Convention and Visitors Bureau, the Geysers Geothermal Association, and the wine industry. Beginning in 1987 KFTY began actively selling its video-production services. Presently the crew of KFTY Productions turns out three or four videos per month.

Consistent with its original purpose of addressing community/ regional interests, Channel 50 responds immediately to news stories of local concern, such as the Russian River flood of 1986. Television as a medium is prepared for the unexpected. KFTY is the only regional news medium that covers all six counties of Sonoma, Marin, Solano, Napa, Yolo, Lake, and Mendocino.

Scores of plaques that cover the wall adjacent to the entrance are evidence of the station's active role in the local community. KFTY has been an involved participant in many regional efforts: helping establish the Luther Burbank Center for Arts, assisting the Salvation Army in establishing a safe house, and supporting a theatrical production to raise funds for the homeless. When the model of the Vietnam Memorial came to the area, KFTY reunited three veterans, each of whom thought the other two had been killed in the war.

KFTY has established an intern program with regional colleges to give students hands-on experience in the television industry. Originally intended to help students with career decisions, the program has supplied the station with many of its present employees who were once participants in the program.

When it began in 1981, Channel 50 employed 35 people and was on the air 10 hours each day, seven days per week. After only eight years its employees have doubled to 70, and it currently is on the air 24 hours per day, seven days per week. The station's success is testimony to the ability of Wishard Brown and his staff to meet the challenges incumbent with establishing an independent station in an area already served by nationally affiliated stations nearby.

Patrons

The following individuals, companies, and organizations have made a valuable commitment to the quality of this publication. Windsor Publications and the Sonoma County Historical Society gratefully acknowledge their participation in *Sonoma County: The River of Time.*

Berry's Sawmill, Inc.*
Gloria Ferrer Champagne Caves*
Glen Ellen Winery*
The Great Petaluma Mill and Steamer Gold Landing*

Holiday Inn–Sonoma County Wine Country*
Hunt and Behrens Feed Mill*
Kaiser Permanente Medical Center*
KFTY-Television Channel 50*
Price Pump Company*
Red Lion Hotel*
The Sea Ranch*
Sears Point International Raceway*
Serres Corporation*
Shamrock Materials, Inc.*
Sonoma County Museum*
Sonoma State University*
John Tate, Inc.*

*Partners in Progress of *Sonoma County: The River of Time.* The histories of these companies and organizations appear in Chapter 8, beginning on page 95.

The former United States Post Office in Santa Rosa is now the home of the Sonoma County Museum. Courtesy, Sonoma County Museum

Bibliography

Adams, Leon D. *The Wines of America.* New York: McGraw-Hill, 1978 and 1985.

Alexander, James B. *Sonoma Valley Legacy; Histories and sites of 70 historic adobes.* Sonoma Valley Hisorical Society, 1986.

Alt, David D., and Donald W. Hyndman. *Roadside Geology of Northern California.* Missoula: Mountain Press Publishing Co., 1981.

Bailey, Floyd P. *Santa Rosa Junior College, 1918-1957: A Personal History.* Santa Rosa, 1967.

Bancroft, Hubert Howe. *History of California.* 7 vols. San Francisco: The History Company, 1886.

————. *Register of Pioneer Inhabitants of California 1542 to 1848.* Baltimore: Regional Publishing, 1964.

Barrett, S.A. *Pomo Myths.* Milwaukee: Bulletin of the Public Museum of the City of Milwaukee, V. XV, 1933.

Bauer, Patricia M. "California's First Power Sawmill." *The Timberman* September 1956.

Bean, Walton, and James J. Rawls. *California, an Interpretive History.* New York: McGraw-Hill, 1988.

Benson, Foley. *From Straw into Gold; Selected Basketry Traditions of the American West.* Santa Rosa: Jesse Peter Memorial Museum, 1986.

Bidwell, John. *In California Before the Gold Rush.* Los Angeles: Ward Ritchie Press, 1948.

Bronstein, Zelda, and Kenneth Kann. "Basha Singerman, Comrade of Petaluma." *California Historical Society Quarterly* Spring 1977.

Brown, Vinson, and Douglas Andrews. *Pomo Indians of California and Their Neighbors.* Healdsburg: Naturegraph Publishers, 1969.

Bunje, Emil, and Frederick Schmitz. *Russian California 1805-1841.* Berkeley: U.S. Works Progress Administration, 1937.

Canillo, Alexis. *The Lonely Valley.* Santa Rosa Indian Center Heritage Project, 1980.

Carrillo, Alma McDaniel, and Eleanora Carrillo deHaney. *History and Memories: The Carrillo Family in Sonoma County.*

Clar, C. Raymond. *Out of the River Mist.* Santa Cruz, California: Forest History Society, 1973.

Cloverdale Then and Now, Being a History of Cloverdale, California, Its Environs, and Families. Cloverdale, 1982.

"The Coast Rangers: A Chronicle of Events in California," *Harper's New Monthly Magazine* July 1861.

Cowan, G. Robert. *Ranchos of California; a list of Spanish Concessions 1775-1822 and Mexican grants 1822-1846.* Fresno: Academy Library Guild, 1956.

Cross, Ralph Herbert. *The Early Inns of California 1844-1869.* San Francisco: Cross and Brandt, 1954.

DeClerq, John H. *A History of Rohnert Park: From Seed to City.* Rohnert Park, 1976.

DeTurk, Isaac. *Vineyards in Sonoma County.* Sacramento: Board of State Viticultural Commission, 1893.

Dickinson, A. Bray. *Narrow Gauge to the Redwoods.* Trans-Anglo Books, 1970.

Dillon, Richard. *The Story of The Sea Ranch.* Oceanic Properties, 1965.

Dreyer, Peter. *A Gardener Touched with Genius: The Life of Luther Burbank.* Berkeley: University of California Press, 1985.

Duflot de Mofras, Eugene. *Travels on the Pacific Coast.* Santa Ana: Fine Arts Press, 1937.

Dutton, Joan Parry. *They Left Their Mark: Famous passages through the wine country.* St. Helena: Illuminatons Press, 1983.

Exploration du territoire de l'Oregon des Californies, et de la mer vermeille. Paris: Arthus Bertrand, 1844.

Finley, Ernest L. *History of Sonoma County, California; Its People and Its Resources.* Santa Rosa: Press Democrat Publishing Co., 1937.

Gibson, James R. *Imperial Russia in Frontier America.* New York: Oxford University Press, 1976.

————. "Russian Expansion in Siberia and America," in *Russia's American Colony,* S. Frederick Starr, ed. Durham: Duke University Press, 1987, pp. 32-40.

Golovnin, V. M. *Around the World on the Kamchatka, 1817-1819.* Honolulu: Hawaiian Historical Society, 1979.

Gregory, Tom. *History of Sonoma County, California with Biographical Sketches.* Los Angeles: Historic Record Co., 1911.

"The Gregson Memoirs." *California Historical Society Quarterly* Vol. XIX, 1940, p. 113-143.

Handbook of North American Indians., Vol. 8.

Robert F. Heizer, volume editor. Washington, D.C.: Smithsonian Institution, 1978.

Hansen, Harvey. *People on the Land: The Last Days of Fort Ross.* (videotape)

————, and Jeanne Thurlow Miller. *Wild Oats in Eden: Sonoma County in the 19th Century.* Santa Rosa, 1962.

Haraszthy, Agostin. *Father of California Wine: Agostin Haraszthy, with Grape Culture, Wines and Wine-Making.* Santa Barbara: Capra Press, 1979.

Heizer, Robert F. *Elizabethan California.* Ramona, California: Ballena Press, 1974.

————. *They Were Only Diggers; A Collection of Articles from California Newspapers 1851-1866, on Indian and White Relations.* Ramona, California: Ballena Press, 1974.

————, and Albert B. Elsasser. *The Natural World of the California Indians.* Berkeley: University of California Press, 1980.

Hine, Robert V. *California's Utopian Colonies.* New York: W.W. Norton, 1966.

Historical Atlas Map of Sonoma County California. Oakland: Thomas H. Thompson & Co., 1877.

Hoffman, Ogden. *Reports of Land Cases Determined in the U.S. District Court for Northern District of California, 1852-1858.* Vol. I, 1862.

Ide, Simeon. *The Conquest of California: A Biography of William B. Ide.* Oakland: Biobooks, 1944.

Illustrated History of Sonoma County, California. Chicago: Lewis Publishing Co., 1889.

Jackson, Walter A. *Doghole Schooners.* Volcano, California: California Travelers, Inc., 1969.

Khlebnikov, Kyrill T. *Colonial Russian America, 1817-1832.* Portland, Oregon: Oregon Historical Society, 1976.

Kneiss, Gilbert H. *Redwood Railways: A Story of Redwoods, Picnics and Commuters.* Berkeley: Howell-North, 1956.

Kroeber, A.L. *Handbook of the Indians of California.* New York: Dover Publications, 1976. (Reprint of Bureau of American Ethnology of the Smithsonian Institution, Bulletin 78, GPO, Washington, D.C., 1925).

Latimer, Patricia. *California Wineries, Vol. 2: Sonoma and Mendocino.* Saint Helena: Vintage Image, 1976.

Le Baron, Gaye, and Dee Blackman, Joann

Mitchell, and Harvey Hansen. *Santa Rosa, A Nineteenth Century Town.* Santa Rosa: Historia, Ltd., 1985.

Lee, Hector. *Tales of California.* 1974.

MacMullen, Jerry. *Paddle-Wheel Days in California.* Palo Alto: Stanford University Press, 1944.

Marchand, Alexis. Unpublished letters to and from the Icarian Community, Sonoma County. California Historical Society Library, San Francisco.

Margolin, Malcolm. *The Way We Lived; California Indian Reminiscences, Stories and Songs.* Berkeley: Heyday Books, 1981.

Marryat, Frank. *North Bay Journal and Visits to Gold Rush San Francisco.* Santa Rosa: Clio Publications, 1977. (Reprinted from first edition, 1855.)

McKee, Irving. "Historic Sonoma County Winegrowers." *California, The Magazine of the Pacific* September 1955.

McKittrick, Myrtle M. *Vallejo, Son of California.* Portland: Binfords and Mort, 1944.

Mullen, Barbara Door. *Sonoma County Crossroads.* San Rafael, 1974.

Munro-Fraser, J.P. *History of Sonoma County, California, Illustrated.* Aley, Bowen & Co., 1880. (Reprinted by Petaluma: C.B. Veronda, 1973.)

The New Shasta Daisies. Santa Rosa: Burbank's Experiment Farms, 1904.

Noto, Sal. "Homage to Jack London: The House of Happy Walls," *Pacific Historian* Summer 1978.

O'Brien, Bickford, ed. *Fort Ross: Indians, Russians, Americans.* Jenner: Fort Ross Interpretive Association, 1980.

O'Brien, Robert. "The Passing of the Petaluma." *Riptides* August 30 and September 1, 4, and 6, 1950.

Parmalee, Robert D. *Pioneer Sonoma.* Sonoma: The Sonoma Index-Tribune, 1972.

Pastel, Consuelo M. *Loss of Property of the Japanese During World War II.* Sonoma State University, 1979.

Payeras, Fr. Mariano. *Travels of the Canon Fernandez de San Vincente to Ross.* Bancroft Manuscript Collection MS C-C18, pp. 411-428. Nicholas Del Cioppo, California Dept. of Parks and Recreation, translator and editor, August 1979.

Pelanconi, Joseph D. *Quicksilver Rush of Sonoma County, 1873-75.* Chico, California: Chico State College M.A. Thesis, 1969.

Perez, Cris. *Grants of Land in California Made by Spanish or Mexican Authorities.* State Lands Commission.

Phillips, Linda. *Impact of Rail Transportation on Urban Geography of Santa Rosa, California 1854-1906.* Master's Thesis prepared for Sonoma State University, 1986.

Reed, Anna M. "Prohibition is Piracy." Petaluma: Northern Crown, January 1916.

Report to Mariano G. Vallejo: Confidential Information Concerning the Ross Settlement, 1833. Nicholas Del Cioppo, California Dept. of Parks and Recreation, editor and translator, August 1979.

Robinson, W.W. *Land in California.* Berkeley: University of California Press, 1948.

Roddy, W. Lee. *Black Bart and Other California Outlaws,* 1970.

Rolle, Andrew. "Italians in California." *Pacific Spectator* Autumn 1955.

Sail and Steam on the Northern California Coast, 1850-1900. Compiled by Wallace E. Martin. San Francisco: National Maritime Museum Association, 1983.

Seventy-Five Years of Presbyterianism 1855-1930. Santa Rosa.

Shutes, Milton. "Fighting' Joe Hooker." *California Historical Society Quarterly* 1937, pp. 304-320.

Smith, John Stephen. *Sonoma County Exiles: The Japanese-Americans and World War II.* Sonoma State University, 1975.

Sonoma County Economic Development Board. *Agribusiness Summary.* December 1984.

Speth, Frank Anthony. *A History of Agricultural Labor in Sonoma County, California.* Master's Thesis, University of California, 1938.

Stevenson, Robert Louis. *The Silverado Squatters.* San Francisco: Grabhorn Press, 1952. (Reprint of 1883 edition.)

Stindt, Fred A. *Trains to the Russian River.* 1974.

Tays, George. "Mariano Guadalupe Vallejo and Sonoma." *California Historical Society Quarterly* V. 16: 99-121, 216-55, 348-72; V. 17: 50-73, 141-67, 219-42.

Thompson, Robert A. *Conquest of California.* Santa Rosa: Sonoma Democrat Publishing Company, 1896.

————. *Historical and Descriptive Sketch of Sonoma County, California.* Philadelphia: L.H. Everts & Co., 1877.

Truffaut, Francois. *Hitchcock.* New York: Simon and Schuster, 1967.

Trussell, Margaret E. *Settlement of the Bodega Bay Region.* Master's Thesis, University of California, 1960.

Tuomey, Honoria. *History of Sonoma County, California.* 2 vols. Chicago: S.J. Clarke, 1926.

U.S. Works Progress Administration. *Sonoma County History and Description.* Compiled by Dorothy Wolf, Richard Brooks, and Albert A. Pond, Santa Rosa, 1936.

U.S. Works Progress Administration. *Foreign Born in Sonoma County.* Compiled by Richard Brooks and Dorothy Wolf, Santa Rosa, 1936.

Willson, Carolyn. "London Album: a California Legend at Work and Play." *California Historical Quarterly* Fall 1976.

The World Encompassed by Sir Francis Drake, carefully collected out of the notes of Master Francis Fletcher. London: printed for Nicholas Bourne, 1628. (Reprinted by Readex Microprint Corp., 1966.)

Index